THE INFORMATIVE GOD

BRAD BOWINS, MD

GAME CHANGER
PUBLICATIONS

ABOUT THE AUTHOR

Dr Bowins is a psychiatrist, researcher, and founder of The Centre For Theoretical Research in Psychiatry & Clinical Psychology. His research and writings challenge the status quo, fostering paradigm shifts so crucial to the advancement of science and knowledge. Several theoretical perspectives, presented in peer-reviewed publications, have advanced the way that key aspects of mental illness are understood. Unique approaches to additional topics, including sexual orientation, men's health, motion sickness, and how consciousness evolved on the basis of time distinctions, also characterize his published works. This same passion for exploring novel themes is carried forward in The Informative God, producing one of the most informed takes on spiritual matters!

OTHER BOOKS BY DR BRAD BOWINS
BOWINSBOOKS.COM

DEFINING MENTAL ILLNESS
CONTINUUMS, REGULATION, AND DEFENSE

OUTING THE TRUTH ABOUT SEXUAL ORIENTATION

AT THE TIPPING POINT
HOW TO SAVE US FROM SELF-DESTRUCTION

VASECTOMY
THE CRUELEST CUT OF ALL
(THE MODERN MEDICAL NIGHTMARE OF POST-VASECTOMY PAIN SYNDROME)

Copyright 2018 by Brad Bowins

For information about permissions to reproduce selections from this book write to Game Changer Publications, PO Box 43, Lindsay, Ontario, Canada, K9V 4R8

ISBN: 978-1-7752600-0-4

Game Changer Publications
PO Box 43
Lindsay, Ontario, Canada
K9V 4R8

DEDICATION

Dedicated to the curious who seek answers beyond what the status quo perspective of the time offers.

THE

INFORMATIVE

GOD

CONTENTS

CHAPTER	PAGE
SECTION 1: THE HORROR	
THAT FATEFUL DAY	2
A SHOOTING STAR	6
SECTION 2: THE CURIOSITY	
AN EGYPTIAN START	12
ISLAM	30
JUDAISM	43
CHRISTIANITY	55
ANCIENT GREEK RELIGION	69
ANCIENT ROMAN RELIGION	79
MAYA RELIGION	88
INCA RELIGION	99
ANISHINAABE AND OBJIBWE RELIGION	111
HINDUISM	119
BUDDHISM	131

CONTENTS

CHAPTER	PAGE
SECTION 3: THE DISCOVERY	
INFORMATION BUT NO ANSWERS	145
TORAJANS: IS DEATH THE END?	151
A HEAVENLY PARADISE	164
IMMORTALITY ACTUALIZED	184
POSTSCRIPT	203

SECTION 1

THE HORROR

THAT FATEFUL DAY

Maybe it was a premonition, or maybe just motion sickness, but I was not feeling good on the bus ride from Vancouver to Whistler along the Sea-to-Sky Highway. By the time I collected my luggage at the airport and located my transportation, only a few rear seats were left, my preference being at the very front for the view and a less queasy ride. Ever since childhood I've been vulnerable to this most evil of conditions, robbing those afflicted of much of the enjoyment that travel brings. Medications work well, if I'd remembered to pack some in my carry-on bag, instead of with my skis and clothes now in the belly of the bus.

    A woman next to me would normally be nice, and the single late forties woman seems very pleasant. At barely thirty most women, even younger, find me attractive, often attributed to my strong symmetrical facial features, and athletic muscular build. Joan is fit for her age and appealing, but my focus is on the skiing to come and not romance, at least not from the get go. In addition, the sensations I'm experiencing are not compatible with romance, nor conversation. Unfortunately, Joan started talking from the moment I boarded the bus, and it appears that she won't stop until we reach Whistler, if even then. As a recently certified physician in internal medicine I need a break from talking, and skiing is the ticket. However, I clearly am not going to get a break from talking on the bus ride to the slopes.

    During the more everyday topics my mind drifted off into fantasy about the skiing to come. Life is all up-hill, while skiing all downhill; this reversal of the normal relentless grind of life making the sport so appealing. I can even feel the turns down a wide-open mogul run with the sun shining, although at Whistler with its wet weather perhaps this is too much fantasy.

Joan's voice intruded on my fantasy escape, "Did you feel that?"

"Feel what?" Having been absorbed in my action fantasy I couldn't discern anything unusual.

"The bus seemed to slide."

"These drivers know what they're doing." I'm eager to return to my ski fantasy.

"Maybe I'll make a quick prayer to the Sea-to-Sky God."

The religious slant more than the tension in her tone surprised me, as I would never have pegged her for being the spiritual type.

I was about to suggest that a prayer might help, not due to any religious motivation, more to stop her talking for a few minutes, when I too felt an unsteady motion that immediately ramped up my odd feeling. Then in a breath the roof became ground and the floor sky. In a panicked millisecond, I realized that the bus had hit the guardrail and flipped over it. What happened next became a defining moment in my life, like no other.

For a brief moment gravity did not seem to work, as I recall being suspended in my seat, looking ahead at a sea of passengers likewise defying gravity. As the laws of the universe caught up I felt myself falling, but not before grabbing hold of the seat ahead of me applying a death grip. I sensed Joan falling away, as were the other passengers. The bus hitting the ground seemed to coincide with everyone landing on the upended roof, because the force snapped necks and crushed spines. Although I can't be sure, I believe the sound of these fractures rose above that of buckling metal. Oddly there were hardly any screams, everything happening so fast, although I had the sense of time slowing to a crawl. Unable to resist the force of the impact I fell, but my strong grip twisted me such that I landed sideways on a cushion of passengers. Surprisingly, it felt less painful than a typical fall while skiing. The only pain, if it could be called that relative to what others were experiencing, consisted of a few bee stings on my hands, likely from all the flying glass that was imbedding itself in flesh.

The next segment of the real-life horror came when the upended bus slammed into something, undoubtedly a large rock or wall. The bodies slid forward in a wave that peaked as they piled up. Sliding with the wave I tried to grab anything, only able to hold onto a couple of people below. Before hitting the seats now above us, I felt a few bodies pass over me. From whatever speed to zero in milliseconds should have ended my life, but the bodies that passed over buffered my impact, and then as the seats wrenched free from the strain I slid along the carpet of people. Falls from sports reminded me to protect my head with arms tight over both sides. Then it all came to an end, or for me a start.

The strangest sensation was the absence of any pain, other than a few points of soreness that I knew would be bruising, and a few small puncture points on my hands from the flying glass. The next oddest sensation being the complete absence of any sound, aside from metal creaking as the bus settled into its grave. No moaning, no screaming, no crying, nothing! Maybe I was dead and only imagining myself alive? Looking to see if my body was lying below with me floating above, I calmed with the realization that I'm part of it still. As the shock settled I began looking at those around me. Nothing, not even work in a trauma center during my training, could have prepared me for the scene, representing one of Dante's deeper levels of hell. Heads were rotated in all degrees other than that compatible with life, and a few even left their body strewn about with blood and tissue seeping out. Suppressing feelings of terror and horror, I looked for a way out. The front was occluded with corpses, as were the sides. The only way out was the rear that a quick look revealed had been wrenched open from the impact. I tried to avoid their faces but the first I noticed was Joan, staring lifelessly past me, her romance and skiing aspirations sadly over.

 Exiting into the light a wave of nausea hit, and I vomited the horror out. With that release, the odd feeling I had at the start of the bus ride vanished. My duty as a physician was to provide medical assistance, but I knew I could never enter that bus, and medical care was for the living. Maybe if I heard any signs of life other than for birds in the surrounding forest. Distancing myself from the dimension of horror I just passed through, I sat on a rock and gazed to the sea. Spontaneously, I uttered, "I'm the only survivor and unscathed!" This revelation triggered a sea of tears and surge of emotions, some positive like relief but most negative. How is it possible that I'm the lone survivor? Is it luck, fate, my quick response grabbing hold of the seat, or just probability that someone would walk away and that someone happened to be me? Why me, though, and not Joan or any of the other passengers? I realize that answers will come later, now there were only questions, and an intensely heightened sense of life.

A SHOOTING STAR

Have you a defining moment in your life? Perhaps an occurrence or revelation that changed everything? "The horror" as I came to call it is my moment, and indeed it seemed not more than a moment, the actual accident only seconds. Following what happened I received more attention than I ever thought feasible, certainly more than my 15 minutes of fame. Emergency responders to the accident assumed that I came to help, and at first refused to believe that I survived the crash. The physics of the event, not to mention pile of corpses, strongly suggested that no one could have survived, or should have survived. It took some convincing, including a mention that my skis and luggage are buried in the bus, although unlikely in any condition that I would want to see, for them to believe my story.

When the media arrived so did stardom. With the cameras shifting between me and the upturned bus, and snippets of corpses to ramp up the interest and shock factor, media had a field day. I was even asked if I was a superhero, my improbable if not impossible survival and muscular build supporting this possibility. I reassured the interviewer that short of surviving an accident that was seemingly impossible to survive, I could not claim any superhero actions, at least not to date. Maybe it was this semi-humorous response that upped my star factor. Waiting her turn impatiently another interviewer asked if I was destined to do something truly great in life, such that some force might have ensured my survival. I responded that this force unfortunately had not shared that special something with me. I refrained from mentioning that if it was destiny how could I possibly know.

Training and practice in medicine with all the questions patients ask was actually proving to be helpful for media interviews. Perhaps the wildest question came from a middle-age male interviewer with no camera backup, asking if this was proof of

God's existence? I later learned that he reported for several Christian publications. He did not appreciate my response that all the other people in the accident would have their doubts.

The next level of stardom came with the radio and television interviews. I was even flown business class to Los Angeles and New York, appearing on prominent talk shows. I avoided the sea of religious media options, simply because there were far too many and I am not a convert. Hosts on more mainstream shows responded well to my, what has been described as fairly dry or dark humor. Stating that my purpose in life is to ensure that Donald Trump rules the planet and possibly the universe, received the best round of laughter. The host rolled with it for days telling his audience I was now employed by "The Donald" to ensure it all came about as destined.

A surprising aspect of these major media interviews is an appreciation of how skilled some of the interviewers actually are. Certainly, they ask the silly and obvious questions, while inserting the more profound ones. One host known more for his sarcastic humor asked, "What do you think this event has to say about the nature of the universe?" Another probed, "Events like yours actually make me wonder if there's a meaning to things. Do you have any idea what that might be?" Not able to answer but intrigued, I caught up with her after the show and did a little of my own probing.

"That question you asked about meaning to things, it seems that you've asked yourself the same question." Not getting any sign that this was not the case I continued, "Can you share any answer or solution?"

"In all these years of doing interviews and hearing stories, it seems that most things are random or via connections, like performers with careers launched and supported by powerful people, but there are times like with you where I'm not so sure. I mean think of the odds against you surviving, and without any injury worth mentioning. How could that be, what are the odds? I don't have any answers but have seen enough to appreciate that there's a real question here."

In the past stars were cultivated over time, movie studios and handlers grooming them. Nowadays stardom is more like shooting stars flaring up in the sky and fading fast, often really fast. My media career went the same way, sought out for interviews and then oblivion. At least I had a life to go back to. During my days in the heavens, grieving the event and death of my fellow passengers was limited, not so much that I was avoiding it. Most physicians come to appreciate how important it is for people to grieve losses. Maybe it was that I didn't know anyone on the bus other than Joan, and she would barely qualify as a relationship. More likely, the relentless demands of my brief stardom kept me buoyed up, and maybe talking about "the horror" was a form of grieving.

Back on the job, doing a locum covering for an internal medicine specialist on leave, I tried to gain some psychological distance from what occurred. Of course, it didn't help that every new patient, and many returning ones, reminded me with statements like, "Oh you're that superhero!" and "Maybe saving me is that special thing you've been kept alive for," followed by a hacking cough, undoubtedly from the three packs of cigarettes smoked per day. I suggested that getting him to stop smoking might qualify. "Ah Doc, nice try." Some of the more thoughtful comments triggered thoughtful reflection. One elderly lady asked, "Have you considered that your role in life might be different, maybe to help us sort out what is really happening?" I pursued my career because it seemed to fit, but maybe there is something more to be done in my life.

    I recalled doing cardiac resuscitation on a middle-age man during my medical residency. All the experience I acquired at chest compressions paid off that day, because they helped to save the patient. However, the part that came to mind, that I'll never forget, is how due to the perfect chest compressions, he not only returned from the dead, but became conscious starting to talk! Understandably his first words were, "What's this?" What followed was more striking, "No let me go back, it's so peaceful. I was leaving and saw you over me." Shocked I stopped the compressions and he became unconsciousness, and likely dead again, until I resumed the compressions, and the medications plus defibrillation restored a normal heart rhythm. He only regained consciousness several hours later. Afterwards, I questioned him about the event, but he only recalled the peacefulness and floating away.

    We drift through life, or more realistically, trip, stumble, and fall through life, with the winners able to get back on their feet, no matter how hard the blow. But is this all there is, only struggle and then death, with a little fun thrown in? There's got to be a meaning or some structure or purpose. But maybe not, after all we do tend to spin things in a positive way, at least those who aren't depressed. Perhaps the meaning is only a positive spin. How nice it would be to exist as an animal, or the non-human type, without any thoughts of meaning beyond survival, reproduction, and looking after offspring. Males of many species do not have to bother with the latter. Idyllic it seems.

    My thoughts became less thoughtful, and more, dare I say mystical. I imagined Joan and the other passengers floating up to the floor of the bus; yes, I know weird. Maybe they were looking down on me and wondering, "Why did he survive?" If they had the peaceful feeling of my resuscitation patient perhaps they were thinking, "That unlucky sod doesn't get to join us yet." Recalling Joan's lifeless gaze, and what would have seemed impossible moments prior to the accident—no talking—it didn't appear that much was happening. We assume that death is completely distinct from life, but is this fully true? I remember reading an article about an Indonesian culture, the name eluding me now, that envision a gradual transition between life and death. They preserve bodies and do not bury them, at least not right away, talking to them as if still alive. A more gradual form of grieving, no doubt, but have they caught onto something we missed? In medicine, it's well known that when a person dies, organs fade at different rates, and even brain structures tend to decay unevenly. There are examples of people being in cold water and resuscitated after hours. These people often report a peaceful feeling, like my resuscitation patient, but I recall reading that others have more nightmare-like experiences. It can't simply be leaving for a better place then.

Over several months my curiosity grew, gradually at first, and building speed like an express train on a level grade. What at first was a vague notion crystallized into a powerful and clear motivation—I have to explore the meaning of life and death, and the nature of the afterlife, if there is one. Sounds good, and I certainly would not be the first to try, nor I'm sure the last. However, we all have to take the direction in life that feels right, and this one does. Who knows, maybe I'm destined to solve the mystery? Of course, the devils in the details, and there were a lot of details to sort out, not the least being how to start and approach the quest. Research has to be the key. If you want to get to the heart of the matter, you have to do your homework, as simple as that. So few people bother, but this is one of the reasons I ended up in medical school and succeeded. Even though the focus will be different now, I have a broad enough background to feel confident approaching any problem, and a diverse range of knowledge is going to be required for sure. I also resolve to write up my research, even if it doesn't lead to an answer, as the journey itself should be interesting. Who knows with a little luck, or fate, I'll satisfy my curiosity.

SECTION 2

THE CURIOSITY

AN EGYPTIAN START

Deciding to seek the truth, and the big answer to the biggest of questions—What is life/death and the afterlife all about—is easier than deciding where to start. Not being a scholar of religion is a minus in that I have not a clue, while a plus in that I do not harbor any preconceived notions. Complete objectivity is an illusion, but relative objectivity and not subjectivity is possible, if there is no preformed idea to defend and seek evidence in support of. Appreciating that ideas often build upon others, the best starting point seems to be an early civilization with no shortage of answers, well understood in the present, and the best example I can think of is ancient Egypt. Ever since seeing those Brendan Fraser movies—The Mummy and its sequel—I imagined ancient Egypt to be an interesting place to live. Of course, movie depictions are not always so realistic.

Landing in Cairo mid-day quickly demonstrated how cultures come and go. Waiting for my luggage the Islamic Call to Prayer broke out over the scratchy ancient public address system. Around me people started to kneel down, although many Egyptian businessmen appeared more annoyed that the luggage carousel wouldn't be loaded until this interruption is over. Despite the scratchiness of the sound there is an inspiring, almost transcendental, quality to it. I imagine it serving as a replacement to coffee throughout the day, but from what I understand coffee is popular in the Middle East. The Call to Prayer seemed to arouse and motivate, because following it the luggage arrived on the carousel in no time at all.

    A carry-over from the days of ancient Egypt appears to be no fear of death, judging by the way my taxi driver and those around him navigate the roads of Cairo. If traffic is jammed on two lanes, no problem, just make a third or even fourth. Traffic lights don't even seem to matter, a red apparently signaling for more aggressive driving. A colleague who visited Egypt warned me not to rent a car and I now understand why. Applying some humor, if for no other reason than to reduce my own fear, I commented to the cabbie how it appears that all the drivers must have made their peace with death. Laughing he explained in broken English that nothing, absolutely nothing, stops Cairo traffic, and certainly not traffic lights. Pulling up to the hotel I'm feeling very thankful to still be alive, not yet having made my peace with death.

A major plus of travel to Egypt is no rain. No worries of booking that trip you've always wanted to go on and it raining for 6 out of 7 days, clearing on your last day. It just doesn't rain. I read that over 95% of the country is desert with people settling a narrow ribbon along the Nile, and the delta region where the Nile discharges into the Mediterranean. Isolated settlements also occur along the Red Sea, such as Hurghada to the west and Sharm El Sheikh on the Sinai Peninsula, the latter an engineered vacation and scuba destination. Cairo is located on the northern section of the Nile sprawled over an increasingly large area.

My starting point in the quest for an answer is appropriately a starting point for ancient Egypt—The step pyramid of Djoser outside of Cairo at Saqqara. Deciding that there is greater safety in numbers, not from terrorists but from Cairo drivers, I opted for the mini-van excursion. Ensuring the foremost seat also ensured no motion sickness. The narrative by the guide, who thankfully did not have to drive at the same time, leaving that to his companion, proved to be very informative.

Apparently, the temple complex we are about to see at Saqqara established Memphis as the capital of the Old Kingdom of Egypt. Around 2600 BC the ruler Djoser had a step pyramid constructed to aid his journey in the afterlife, once he died of course. A truly multi-talented person under him, Imhotep, architect, physician, priest, and founder of a healing cult (quite a resume), designed something never seen before—A 6-step pyramid based on the prior rectangular mastaba design. However, since the mud-brick mastaba tomb would never support additional layers, Imhotep used carved stone to ensure that the structure would support itself, and also the numerous passageways below to be used by King Djoser in his afterlife. The passageways were designed to fool tomb robbers, but did not really work as the tomb was raided and the treasures stolen.

Apparently shaken from a hypnotic absorption in the game on his phone, a young teenager with a cap reading "Mummies Rock," interrupted the engrossing narrative, "Imhotep's that dude who went after Brendan Fraser, and almost wiped out Egypt!"

Demonstrating good social skills, and likely experience with not well-read teenagers, the guide commented, "Yes, I believe he also did that, and did so well at everything he became a God himself later on."

"That's chill. Maybe if I come up with a great idea, I'll become one," as he returned to the focus on the phone game.

"Anything's possible." The guide's nice summation evoking laughter ignored by the teenager, his renewed focus in the game so absolute.

Shortly after this humorous interlude the mini-van pulled into the parking lot. A side benefit of the terrorism threat is that the number of tourists has dropped to a manageable level according to the guide. Apparently, tour vans were almost stacked like step pyramids prior to this nasty era.

Awe and almost shock are my reactions entering the temple complex: I expected not much more than the pyramid, instead discovering that it lies at one end of a rectangle, consisting of a central courtyard surrounded by temple buildings.

Noting the impressed looks on the faces of his charges, our guide exclaimed, "Fit for a king, isn't it?" Affirmative nods followed. "Ancient Egyptians never did anything small, as you can see."

"So long ago too, I doubt many countries could build something like this now. There must not have been any shortage of slaves." I couldn't resist the commentary.

"Ah, you raise a key point I was going to get to, the labor force. Early on in Egyptian history kings were closer to Gods, some say God-Kings, and as such controlled much of the world's money. Sort of like now with the elite billionaires who feel entitled to the wealth of Gods. However, God-Kings like Djoser actually created enduring legacies, instead of hiding in the shadows and monopolizing money." I'm pleased to see that our guide shares my perspective on the ludicrous monopolization of wealth plaguing the modern world.

"Djoser did not have to use slaves, instead he paid for all this with countless workers, many highly skilled craftsmen, having employment. Sort of redistributing some of the wealth. As the years passed Egyptian rulers had to share more and more of the wealth, and about a thousand years after Djoser they could no longer afford to build pyramids. Burials then occurred in the Valley of Kings near Luxor, or ancient Thebes. For some reason, we seem to be going in the opposite direction nowadays. Who knows, we might even return to pyramids for deceased multi-billionaires!"

A tour guide speaking his mind, as opposed to some sterilized presentation. I like it. "Life's always a competition, isn't it?"

"It certainly is, and speaking of competitions does anyone have any idea what occurred in this large space?"

"Chariot races with gladiators," piped in the teenager, his parents pretending to examine a statue away from him.

"Actually, not that far off, although Roman gladiators came a bit later. There was at least one major festival per year, and as part of it, Djoser raced on foot against other men. He ruled for at least 19 years, and as he got older, and probably larger, the race must have slowed to a crawl, since he had to win. Anyone deciding to pass him likely would have visited the afterlife pretty fast. Even as a God-King he could not slow the impact of aging."

Perhaps hoping to show that the entire family was not cursed with their son's video game historical knowledge, his mother stated, "I read that the ancient Egyptians had several Gods and not just one."

"Yes, that's absolutely spot on. They were polytheistic, meaning they believed in several Gods, as opposed to monotheistic, like Islamic, Jewish, and Christian faiths, believing in one God. The ancient Egyptians worshipped many different deities representing the various forces of nature. The system was complex and evolving. The ancient Greeks and Romans also believed in many Gods, as do most aboriginal peoples. A belief in "a God" is more of an anomaly. The Gods of ancient Egypt controlled virtually all aspects of the world, and by worshipping them you could gain favor, or that was the idea."

"So historically multiple Gods were the norm?" The teenager's father likely wanted to demonstrate that his son's limited grasp of history did not arise from his side of the family.

"Yes, hard to believe in this era of one God, but there you have it. The ancient Egyptians represented the normal belief system, although they were the best and most creative, and they also excelled by documenting it on temple walls and papyrus writings. How many of you have seen or are going to see other temples?" When everyone raised their hand, he continued, "Then you have or will learn more of the various Gods and how they changed in popularity over time."

The remainder of the tour consisted of a walk around the complex examining carved depictions of life at the time, and portrayals of Djoser's accomplishments, real and embellished, qualifying him as a God-King. According to our guide, many of the most impressive depictions are in the chambers below, but given the questionable stability of the underground passages only researchers and engineers are allowed in. Apparently Djoser was not enough of a God to prevent deterioration in his step pyramid. The guide explained that the pyramid was initially covered in brilliant white limestone rock, that would have made the structure literally glow in the sun, but this had long since broken down. Still not bad at all for thousands of years old!

I realize that ancient Egypt alone is going to provide a great deal of information that might shed light on the big answer, and I'm only starting my exploration of its contribution. The next stop in my journey, reserved for tomorrow afternoon, is the Great Pyramids of Giza.

It's interesting how fast we adjust to circumstances we find ourselves in, because on the way to the hotel I barely noticed the weaving through Cairo traffic. Back home I'll probably lose my driver's license in a month if I get too used to the Cairo driving style. Enquiring about the legalities in Egypt our guide informed us that "tipping" for favors is common in the region, and with traffic offences avoids the hassles of court and the like. The traffic police actually rely on it to supplement their meager salaries. The name applied to it is "baksheesh," a nicer term than bribery. He further explained that it eases social tensions, as it helps to spread the wealth around, so if someone offers to help with your bag, they are not trying to steal it, they just want a very small piece of the pie. You learn something every day.

How amazing it would have been to live in ancient Egypt and see the pyramids being constructed. This thought popped into my mind the second the tour van arrived at the Great Pyramids of Giza in the early afternoon. Of course, working in the open sun could not have been too much fun. Gazing back at the outskirts of Cairo presented the best argument yet against sprawl development. As the population of Cairo mushrooms construction has arrived on the doorstep of the pyramids, and signs for Coca-Cola and Burger King are there for the deceased Kings of Egypt to see. I imagined them turning over in their graves, and thinking of a curse aimed at developers. At least Cairo developers haven't applied bribery, sorry baksheesh, to convince Cairo officials to clear the pyramids away for development.

My focus shifted back to the pyramids with the sound of loud snorting. A herd of camels led by a very ancient looking Egyptian approached our group. Tacky, yes for sure, but fun to have a camel ride to the pyramids. My camel goes by the name of Brittany Spears. Bouncing along on this very uneven ride, I can appreciate the sacrifice of those early desert traders, and also the awe that must have been felt when they arrived at these great structures. Photos give an image of the pyramids, but not a feel for their size, and how they dwarf human life, something the makers must have realized.

Shortly, we arrived at the base of the largest pyramid. Our guide, a different one than the prior day, explained that a fourth-dynasty king, Sneferu, who ruled from 2,686 to 2,667 BC, started the modern pyramid design. His first pyramid at Medum began as a step one like that of Djoser, and was modified to be a true pyramid. It was unstable, though, and the limestone blocks began to slip. The next attempt at Dahshur started with the right idea—a true pyramid—but the corners were built on unstable ground resulting in shifting and cracking. To compensate, the upper section was constructed with a lesser incline resulting in a bent pyramid. You can only imagine the building contractor trying to explain that one. Maybe a lesser price, or simply avoiding being buried alive in it. Obviously not one to give up, King Sneferu persisted and got it right a mile away with what's called the Red Pyramid, named due to the use of red limestone.

King Sneferu's son, King Khufu, undoubtedly relieved that his father had solved the basic engineering problems, built the first great pyramid at Giza. Construction took about 20 years with paid workers, up to 100,000 at a time, employed during the seasonal flooding of the Nile when it was impossible to farm. Over 2 million massive limestone blocks were used, and the outer surface was coated in smooth limestone. Unfortunately, to help build Cairo, the outer limestone was removed years ago. Sides are oriented to the four points of the compass with a length of 755 ft., an initial height of 481 ft., and an incline of 51 degrees. These figures sound impressive, but are cold descriptions of a monument to mankind's ingenuity, surging from the flat desert to impress the Gods. Looking up at the peak it actually merges with the sky, seemingly making a point of contact. How could any God not be impressed? Passage into the afterlife for this, no problem, you've earned it!

Perhaps wanting to join his father, King Khafre, built the second largest pyramid. He created the illusion that it's larger than his father's pyramid, by building it on elevated ground, and making the angle slightly steeper. I wonder if King Khafre had father issues? In addition to his pyramid he is credited with building the Great Sphinx, 66 ft. high and 240 ft. long, making it the largest sculpture in the world. It was carved from a limestone outcropping, designed to represent the Sun God, Ra, as he rises in the east at dawn, but the face is that of King Khafre. The nose is gone, due to Napoleon's soldiers using it for target practice in 1798, a real sign of European enlightenment. A walkway extends from the rear of the Great Sphinx to King Khafre's pyramid, and it's not difficult to imagine the elaborate funeral procession along this passage.

King Khafre's own son, King Menkaura, built the smallest of the 3 great pyramids, less than half the height of his grandfather King Khufu's pyramid. These pyramids are the only surviving Seven Wonders of the Ancient World, and are a favorite vacation destination now as they have been since construction. When people think of the Pyramids of Giza and the Great Sphinx it is common to just imagine these structures and nothing else. Instead, it's really a pyramid complex or series of them. There are smaller pyramids and temples, and a rebuilt wooden boat to aid King Khufu in his journey to the afterlife. A solar-powered museum that the Sun God Ra would be impressed with, protects and displays this boat. The elongated and upturned bow sweeps back to a flat section with oars in place as if ready to transport the king. Waterways connected the pyramid complex to the Nile, so it is understandable that the ancient Egyptians would design boats to carry them to the afterlife.

I am rapidly gaining the impression that much of ancient Egyptian religion focuses on what occurs after death. I brought this point up to our guide, "It seems that they were almost obsessed with passage to the afterlife."

"In a sense that's true, but ancient Egyptians saw many connections between this life and the afterlife, with several deities playing a role in both worlds, such as Osiris who is God of the Underworld, and also a fertility God. Their Gods pass between worlds, such as Osiris who after being murdered became God of the underworld. Osiris achieved great popularity in this latter role because it was believed that he would rule people justly after death. You can even see temple reliefs where a recently deceased person appears before Osiris, and if his heart is pure is allowed to proceed to the afterlife."

"What if his heart is not pure?"

"Then a less nice fate awaits that person. Quite a motivator for being good in this world, wouldn't you say?"

"That's for sure."

"To gain favor with the Gods, pharaohs and more common people worshipped them, such as the pharaohs who built these pyramids worshipping the sun God Ra, or Re, as "Sons of Ra." To really gain power, linkages between Gods were worshiped, such as by joining Ra with Amun, the God of hidden powers producing Amun-Ra. Now that's a force to have on your side."

"It appears that there was quite a creative aspect to Egyptian religious beliefs."

"Yes exactly, and that is how it always is: God or Gods are created in mankind's image more than the reverse!"

A member of the tour group, clearly from the deep south of the United States, based on his drawl, evidently offended by this suggestion, piped in, "Ah come on, next thing you'll be saying is that all these fake Gods are still floating around here. I might not agree with them Muslims, but they have it right believing in one God for everything!"

Demonstrating her clearly advanced education our guide responded, "We tend to view things in a way that is consistent with the time we live in, and currently one God is popular. However, mostly throughout history there have been many Gods at a time representing the forces of nature, such as the sun or fertility. People have more recently lumped these different roles under one God."

Unwilling to relinquish his point the man responded, "But one God controlling everything makes more sense, since someone's got to be in charge, like the president."

"You're touching on something that characterizes all religions, and demonstrates how we create God or Gods in our own image—Hierarchies. During our own evolution in hunting-gathering groups over the last 200,000 or so years, we relied on hierarchies for defense and offense. It's like a modern fighting force with leadership doing better than one with no chain of command. The benefit of hierarchies for repelling predators and competing hunting-gathering groups, and also being successful with attacks, was so great that our social cognition ensures that we structure things in a hierarchy, including religious beliefs. I've studied religions of all times and places for my doctorate degree, and can say that there is always a hierarchy to both the Gods, some more powerful than others, and also to rankings within the religion, such as the Pope over Archbishops over Bishops. We project this hierarchical model into all we see, including religious beliefs showing how mankind, or maybe I should say womankind, designs religious beliefs based on our own image."

Sounding less convinced the man replied, "Maybe we see it this way because one God's in charge of everything."

"That's the fun of religion, we just don't know, and can produce any concept we want, something that my ancestors excelled at. For example, Bastet, the Cat-headed Goddess, as the daughter of Ra was seen as having the power to ripen the crops. Anubis, as a black jackal was assigned power over funerals and embalming or mummification. Often symbolism was used, such as black for mummification and the color of fertile soil. The best creation however concerns a universal theme of justice and retribution, and is based on Osiris, his wife Isis, their son Horus, and Seth. This is a great story and much like the Ten Commandments seems designed to convey a moral message.

Seth, also sometimes called Set or Sobek, appropriately symbolized as a crocodile, is said to have killed his brother Osiris, cutting his body into 14 pieces. Anubis appointed the son of Osiris and Isis, Horus, to avenge his father's death. Apparently, Isis restored Osiris to immortal life and they produced their son Horus, symbolized as a falcon-headed God. In an immortal battle, Horus killed Seth cutting his body into 14 pieces. Does anyone get the message?"

Showing more smarts than most would have expected, the one God member of our group replied, "An eye-for-an-eye!"

"Exactly, and the basis of many legal systems. This probably aligns with another key piece of our evolution in hunting-gathering groups—Reciprocity. If your hunt goes well and another person's fails, and you give to them, then they are expected to reciprocate later. As part of our social cognition we believe in fairness and expect things to work in this way. Of course, there are those who deceive taking and not reciprocating, but because we expect fairness they are punished, an eye-for-an-eye."

Suddenly recalling a picture of Horus with a prominent beak and eyes, I excitedly commented, "Those eyes of Horus, must be the eye-for-an-eye, a message to everyone!"

"Yes, indeed, a moral lesson from Horus, the God of the sky, war, and hunting. Since, these Gods live forever the message is replayed from generation to generation. Those of you who are going on the Nile tour from Aswan to Luxor, or the reverse, will see how the temples are really like bill-boards advertising beliefs."

Our guide's last statement intensified my anticipation of the next leg of my Egyptian odyssey on a Nile cruise. Even though there are significant sites from Cairo to Luxor, I was informed that Islamic terrorists are too powerful in this region, and Nile boats carrying tourists might be shot at, hence the Nile cruises are only between Luxor and Aswan. Before the cruise, I visited the Egyptian Museum of Cairo, marveling at the artwork of ancient Egypt. It struck me they were perhaps the most creative people ever, the stories and legends matched by the art they produced. The gold mask of Tutankhamun composed of 11 kg of gold stood out as the most impressive. However, seeing statues of Khafre and other key figures is nearly as fascinating. The so-called mummy room, where under climate controlled conditions important Egyptian pharaohs rest, is impressive in an eerie way. All these powerful figures together for the common person to see. To lighten the aura, I pictured them having a party and discussing old times after the lights went out. Now that's a party to avoid, unless you're a King or Queen.

Arriving at the Old Cataract Hotel in Aswan, I stepped back in time. Not to ancient Egypt, but to the time of Agatha Christie and Death on the Nile. Waiting for my room to be readied, I took a seat on the expansive patio, the old-fashioned wicker chairs fitting perfectly with the ornate railing and lanterns. Although tempted to order a tea and capture the true Agatha Christie experience, I went with a cocktail when the waiter arrived. His old-fashioned Arabic clothing made me wonder if I really have been transported back in time. The white-sailed feluccas passing by Elephantine Island reinforcing the notion of time travel. However, having read up on the area, the calmness of the water reveals that I'm still in my own era. The High Aswan Dam created in the mid-20th century, tamed the cataracts in the area, creating Lake Nasser in the process. The project enables the flow of water along the Nile to be regulated, the disadvantage being that sediments giving the soil its fertility, largely remain trapped on the lake side of the dam.

After getting my room, I spent a relaxing half-day sailing in a felucca captained by a white robbed Egyptian, who spoke barely more English than I did Arabic. That evening I read more about Ancient Egypt, sitting on my small balcony with its view of the Nile. Talk about the Agatha Christie experience, and tomorrow there will be part two with the Nile cruise.

Entering the boat after lunch I encountered a site too amazing for a youngish man without romance for a while: A beautiful woman reclining on her side wearing a short skirt with Egyptian symbols on it, barely noticeable given my focus on her well-tanned legs. A couple of muscular men naked above their waists stood fanning her with palm fronds. I surmise that she is supposed to represent Cleopatra. If so I would have liked to see this historical figure, although somehow, I doubt that her true figure matched that of the woman before me. This cruise is certainly starting off well, and I can see why Islamic terrorists might be taking shots at these boats. They are probably trying to spy the woman through rifle scopes and being too excited squeeze their triggers. I considered asking her for a date, but the musclemen guarding her were a disincentive, much as they would have been in Cleopatra's time.

A key advantage of a Nile cruise for those prone to motion sickness is that there is no motion. The Nile tamed by the High Aswan Dam is as calm as a swimming pool. The size of the boats is reasonable too with about 70 passengers, broken into smaller groups for tours. I was hoping for the Cleopatra impersonator to lead my group, but ended up with a middle-age male guide, Christopher. He explained that the sites we will be visiting prior to arriving at our final destination to the north—Luxor—were all built by the Greeks from about 300 years before Christ to around the time of his life and death; he had no trouble saying this as the boat is owned and staffed by Egyptian Christians who make up less than 10% of the population, the numbers declining as they leave due to persecution. He explained that Romans later added to the monuments, also as a way of paying homage to Egyptian Gods to gain the favor of the local people, an example of bill-board advertising the temple way.

Our first destination, Kom Ombo, started off as a frightening experience for several in our group. Upon stepping off the boat we were "attacked" by Egyptian men selling all sorts of goods. They ignored the boundary markings designed to keep them back, advancing as a wave. Barely surviving the onslaught with only a small amount of money spent, we arrived safely at the temple. The thought of a return to the boat was something I pushed out of mind.

Once Christopher detected that the heart rate and blood pressure of his charges had returned to normal levels, he started his presentation, "What is your impression of the temple?"

"A safe refuge from Egyptian salesmen." I could not resist the comment.

"Yes, in this time and I'm sure in the past as well, but in terms of the temple itself. Look at the depictions."

An insightful elderly woman rose to the occasion, "The two sides seem different, the images aren't the same."

"Exactly! This is the only temple in Egypt dedicated to two Gods, Horus and Seth, also known as Set or Sobek." He then recounted the legend presented by my guide at Giza, followed by, "Seth is the Crocodile-Headed God, while Horus is the Falcon-Headed God. The carved reliefs on both temples show the one God honoring the other, sort of a reconciliation. Kom Ombo is also thought to have been a school of mummification and/or medicine."

Proceeding to a nearby wall he pointed to what could only be medical instruments and a birthing chair. "Embalmers used the long-pointed tool to remove the brain of the deceased through the nose. Interestingly, they never considered the brain to be of much value, and instead preserved the stomach, intestines, lungs, and liver in canopic jars. The heart was most valued, being seen as the seat of the soul and so was left in the body, as it would be needed in the afterlife. Osiris judged the purity of one's heart to determine if passage into the afterlife is to occur."

Further into the tour we came to a pool. "This is where Nile crocodiles were trapped, and latter mummified in honor of Seth." We briefly visited a small temple room nearby displaying mummified crocodiles in glass cases.

At an oddly shaped elongated well he stopped and asked, "Who can guess what this was used for?" Seeing only looks of puzzlement he continued, "For taxes—The more the Nile flooded, the better the crops, and the level of water in this well registered the extent of Nile flooding for the given year. Higher levels meant higher taxes!" Smiling he added, "I suspect that tax-evaders were used to help feed the Nile crocodiles to keep the God Seth satisfied."

Laughter following his hypothesis intensified when I added, "Perhaps a few of those salesmen we encountered could help restore the power and glory of Seth."

"Why didn't I think of that," mused Christopher.

Focusing on a newly arrived group of passengers, the salesmen were so distracted that we slipped by wallets intact on the short walk to the boat. Lunch on the open deck with shading against the relentless sun was a refreshing experience, as was the animated conversation of what was seen and learned. I realize how great Egypt is as a starting point to satisfy my curiosity, because so much infrastructure is in place to learn about the religion of ancient Egypt, and also somewhat those of other cultures. We spent the rest of the day relaxing watching the sites of the Nile pass by, on our way to Edfu. The crew informed us that we will be visiting it tomorrow morning.

Edfu, or the Temple of Edfu seems remarkably intact, as if built yesterday. Our guide explained that it is the second largest temple after Karnak, and dedicated strictly to Horus, the Sky God. The prominent statues of Horus by the entrance sort of give that away. The temple was erected by the Greeks, but built on an earlier temple devoted to Horus. After defeating Seth, the killer of his father Osiris, Horus ruled, although Osiris reportedly reigned from the afterlife. Meanwhile, evil Seth was exiled. Stories of good battling evil are in every culture, but the ancient Egyptians placed it front and center in their religion. The eyes of Horus are also said to represent the sun and moon ensuring a day and night vigil of the sky. Interpretations are the norm as others believe that the sharp sighted prominent eyes of this falcon God emphasize an eye-for-an-eye, and how Horus would not miss sighting a transgression.

One of the most amazing aspects of Edfu is how it demonstrates classic Egyptian architecture, and the hierarchical nature of their society. The entrance consists of a giant pylon, leading to a large courtyard with tall walls, called the Court of Offerings, designed for common people. Next is the Hypostyle Hall, a covered structure with decorated columns, the height less than that of the courtyard. The Festival Hall and Hall of Offerings follow, and finally the low-ceiling Sanctuary reserved for the pharaoh and the most senior priests. A ceremonial barque or barge, that Horus was symbolically carried on during festivals, is still in the Sanctuary. From a side perspective, the temple appears to descend in a series of levels. The higher a person's status the deeper they were allowed to go in the temple.

Reliefs on the temple tell some interesting stories, perhaps the most intriguing and adding a soap opera aspect, is how Hathor the Sky Goddess comes upriver on her sacred barque for an annual meeting with Horus. Who better to get it on with the God of the Sky Horus than the Goddess of the Sky? The story adds a steamy romantic aspect to the temple. More political are the reliefs showing how the Greeks made offerings to Horus, a good publicity stunt to keep the people happy with Greek occupation. Christopher had us turn around when departing and look back at the temple before explaining that it was abandoned after the Roman era, and eventually became entombed in sand. Houses were actually built over it until Auguste Marieete excavated Edfu in the mid 19th century revealing an intact temple, preserved by the dry sand. Fortunately for mankind someone found the temple; unfortunately for the temple the elevated water table from the High Aswan Dam is currently eroding the foundation.

So far, my exploration of Egyptian religion has revealed the fascinating story of Osiris, Isis, Horus, and Seth, and the eye-for-an-eye theme, but how did they come to be in the first place? Doesn't every religion have a creation story? That was next on our itinerary with a visit to the Temple of Esna devoted to the Ram-Headed God Khnum, the God of Creation. I learned that like with Edfu the temple had been buried and was excavated by Auguste Marieete, but this time it was under a built-up city. Largely confined to a narrow ribbon along the Nile, Egyptians over the years have built their structures over previous ones, often using some of the stones for building material. From the Temple of Esna you look up to see the passage of time!

Khnum apparently had a varied and colorful history as a God, starting as a Water God, clearly an important role in a desert. He gave rise to the Nile and ensured that annual flooding deposited enough black silt to make the river banks fertile. The silt was also used for clay, the basis of Egyptian pottery, so Khnum was linked to pottery. One story holds that Khnum molded everything and everyone, including the other Gods, on his potter's wheel. If this was not enough he also created the "First Egg" giving birth to the Sun. Talk about a busy guy! It's said that if you want to get something done give the job to someone who's busy, and that someone seems to have been Khnum. Adding to his roles he was a protector of the dead, with the Book of the Dead, and heart-scarabs buried with people, listing spells to invoke Khnum's assistance. The ram was a very potent animal to the ancient Egyptians, fitting for a God who got so much done. You'd think that he would have been the premier God of ancient Egypt, but after accomplishing so much he was pushed to the sidelines—No respect!

A short distance away from Esna, but quite a long journey given the wait to enter the boat locks, is the ancient city of Thebes, known now as Luxor with the famous temple of Karnak, and the burial sites of the Theban Necropolis on the opposite (west) side of the Nile. Even prepared by the temples visited, the size of Karnak is staggering. It covers over 200 acres with construction extending from the Middle Kingdom around 2,000 years before Christ to the time of the Greeks. Our little group proceeded along an avenue of ram-headed sphinxes, hopefully in honor of Khnum, to the first pylon marking the entrance. Beyond is the courtyard followed by a second pylon leading to the Great Hypostyle Hall, with a forest of 134 columns in 16 rows.

Even today with our advanced machinery it would take forever to construct and decorate this hall, and it had a roof made of stone slabs all those years ago. Maybe Khnum was at work here. However, it appears that another creator God—Amun—stole his fire. Amun referring to invisible, started as a God of air and wind, later becoming a fertility God. He rose to prominence once allied with Ra, becoming Amun-Ra. The Great Hypostyle Hall at Karnak is devoted to Amun-Ra, part of the Temple of Amun-Ra. I am clearly seeing how people created these legends to fit the times and needs of rulers, and also how the one God concept likely evolved to minimize all the confusion. I'm getting a headache trying to sort out even a fraction of the Egyptian Gods. Over many generations Karnak was added to according to our guide, with political motives everywhere to be seen, as with images partially erased or defaced, and the striking pink granite obelisk of Queen Hatshepsut walled off by different rulers. This perfect obelisk rising to the skies must have been too much to stomach for later male rulers desiring greater prominence.

Part two of our Thebe's experience commenced the next day with a visit to the Theban Necropolis, starting with the famous Valley of the Kings. It's like a condo resort of sorts for the dead, with tombs in the cliff faces, the higher and harder to get to ones interning the wealthiest and most important pharaohs. After climbing a long and steep flight of wooden steps, we entered the tomb of Thutmose III. Painted stars cover the ceiling, and in the antechamber a textbook of 740 different divinities is painted on the walls. Amazingly, after all these years the paint is still clear. From the antechamber, the passage makes a sharp turn down a steep tunnel to the burial chamber, where a relief covered sarcophagus lies. Unfortunately, all the precautions didn't deter grave robbers as the treasures were pilfered.

Our group is fortunate because the tomb of King Tut, or properly Tutankhamun, is open to the public. Despite his fame the tomb is very small, and certainly compared to powerful pharaohs such as Thutmose III. He was so relatively insignificant that the entrance to his resting place was buried during construction of a tomb for someone more prominent. Howard Carter, in the late 1800's uncovered the entrance and brought the still sealed in treasures to the world. I recall the gold mask at the Egyptian Museum of Cairo. At this point, Christopher told us a fascinating story.

"The prior ruler, Amenophis IV or Akhenaten, broke with tradition and declared that there was only one state God—Aten—

who apparently was a version of the Sun God Ra, being a visible manifestation of the radiant power of the sun. Temples of other Gods were destroyed, understandably angering priests of these other Gods."

I imagined that with all the Gods there were numerous jobs for priests, and much attrition in the priestly ranks would transpire if there was only one God. Multiple Gods being a form of job security and status. "I suppose a lot of priests would be out of work."

"Exactly, and there was no union to fight for them, so it appears that they took matters into their own hands, ensuring that the child who became king after his father Amenophis IV passed on, restored their job security by getting rid of Aten as the supreme God, and restoring Amun. King Tut's name is actually Tut-Ankh-Amun translating roughly into "I am for Amun," clearly advertising that the old order is back in business. Some suspect that when Tut began to think for himself the priests killed the young ruler, and gave him a quick burial. So much for the God-Kings of Djoser's time."

I recalled seeing a restaurant in Luxor with King Tut's real name. Despite its smaller size, I find King Tut-Ankh-Amun's tomb to be very impressive with the sarcophagus still in residence, apparently holding the actual mummy. Life-like reliefs of baboons also stand out.

Aside from the Valley of the Kings, the Temple of Hatshepsut is the most impressive of the west Nile sites at Luxor, with three levels of terraces cut out of the escarpment, the temple appearing as an extension of the cliff behind it. Statues of Queen Hatshepsut and relief images important to her, such as one of Anubis, add to the amazing architecture. The temple is devoted to Hathor, the Sky-Goddess and lover of Horus, understandable for a female ruler. Her architect and lover, Senenmut, was given the rare reward of having his tomb built on the temple complex, but after a lover's quarrel ended up having to be buried elsewhere. Drama is everywhere and apparently has been throughout time, as it seems to be the human way. In line with all this drama, the early Coptics defaced many of the temple reliefs that offended their sensibilities when they established their own monastery, Deir El Bahri, on the upper terrace.

Feeling somewhat overwhelmed by the information acquired about ancient Egyptian religion and spirituality, the mention of Coptics made me realize that it's time to progress my curiosity to the other principle religions arising in the region. The Middle East certainly is a hot spot for beliefs, with the temples and reliefs as an enduring legacy. Christian (Coptic), Judaism, and Islamic religions, the monotheistic Big 3 as I started calling them, developed in the region. The Islamic religion emerged as the dominant player in the area. It is then fitting to start my monotheistic Big 3 odyssey with an exploration of Islam.

ISLAM

Attempting to understand the various Egyptian Gods and their very different personalities generated an appreciation for the shift to a single God—All that hassle and confusion. Just make one God and simplify things! In our one God world, it's hard to see this motivation, but I can imagine what a relief this must have been to the masses back then. Thank God, instead of Gods, we just have one to learn about. My starting point for monotheism—Islam—is the right one, as no other religion has such an emphasis on the singularity of God, based on what I've heard. Given that I'm still in Luxor, I decided to seek out a mosque in this city. A large jump in time and polytheism to monotheism, but only a short walk from the Nile cruise boat.

    Marveling at the symmetry of the minaret or tower at the top of the mosque, I failed to notice a forties something man approach wearing a white headpiece and black robe. Being influenced by the Western view of how harsh the Islamic religion is, I initially thought he was about to question my presence by the mosque. Wariness rapidly turned to relief and surprise when he smiled. "I am Ahmed, leader of prayers at our mosque. I noticed your interest and wish to invite you in for a tour."

    After introducing myself and explaining how I just completed a Nile cruise I followed him inside. The first impression being the simplicity of the interior—Just a large open space with columns and arches at the sides. No statues or paintings, or really any symbolism.

    Noting my surprise, Ahmed, explained, "Your reaction is typical, because you expect grandeur, is that not so?"

    "Well yes, I suppose, or at least something more space filling."

"With Islam, simplicity and purity are what God represents, and this is reflected in the mosques. The central section is where the faithful kneel and pray, and I as imam lead the prayers."

"What about idols or statues of God?"

"Islam holds that God should not be represented, only worshipped."

Curious about his take on polytheism and monotheism I decided to explore the matter. "In ancient Egyptian religion, many Gods are said to exist, but with Islam, Christianity, and Judaism only one. Why do you think that's so?"

With a twinkle in his eye my pleasant host replied, "Can you get all those Gods straight?" Seeing me nod in understanding he continued, "Our God represents all those Gods in one. We believe in the oneness of God as revealed by the prophet Mohammed."

"But why your God?"

"There is one God for everyone, and all creation comes from this one God. We all belong to a single umma, meaning family or community, and upon death all life goes back to God."

"I understand that the Christian and Jewish faiths with one God came much earlier than Islam, so why the need for another single God faith?"

"For us it really all starts with the prophet Mohammed who was born in Mecca, in what is now Saudi Arabia, in the year 570 after Christ. The people of Mecca at the time believed in several Gods, not being converted to a single God system of belief. While meditating on Mount Hira near Mecca in 610, Mohammed received the first of the revelations from God, brought by the angel Gabriel. This revelation held that there is one God only—Allah in Arabic means, "the God." The people of Mecca did not accept his single God, and experiencing persecution he and his followers fled to Ethiopia. Those with a special message often suffer this fate, but his message did take hold in Yathrib, known later as Medina. More and more tribes accepted his teachings, and eventually Mecca saw the way after battles were waged."

Hoping that I was not appearing skeptical I raised a crucial point. "What gave Mohammed the power to discover this God?"

"Ah my curious friend, it was not Mohammed that had the power, but God revealing himself through Mohammed. It is said that there is no god but God, and Mohammed is the messenger of God!"

"Earlier prophets also claim to have experienced God, so what distinguishes Mohammed?"

"These earlier prophets heard the word of God but it was corrupted. Mohammed heard and recalled the exact words of God, as expressed in the Qur'an. Without fault the Qur'an expresses the word of God. We believe that the Qur'an was kept on a preserved tablet in God's presence, until he revealed it in its entirety to Mohammed."

"That's a lot of information for one person to absorb and recall!"

"Yes, quite a feat, but Mohammed recited the words to those close to him and scribes recorded them. They are as expressed by God. In contrast the bible or versions are interpretations of the word of God, a key difference. That is why the Qur'an cannot be translated into another language."

"Interpret is what people do." I decided to raise a potentially sensitive issue given Ahmed's openness and reasonableness. "If the Qur'an is the word of God how can it be interpreted to support terrorist acts?"

"You have captured the sentiment of true Muslims. It is like Christian's interpreting the bible to support the Crusades many years ago, or acts against other groups. We are all part of a single umma, and not enemy."

"Somehow I don't think that Islamic State and like-minded groups would see it that way."

"As you mentioned people interpret, and often for their own needs; it is this way with all religions. Radical interpretations, as with the leaders of Islamic State, are probably far more motivated by a desire to monopolize power and wealth as by true religious conviction. Those who follow the word of God do not see as their goal the hoarding of wealth and suppression of the weak and vulnerable. Indeed, the Qur'an expresses the value of supporting those in need, including providing to the poor some of what is acquired."

Smiling at my own humor before expressing it I interjected, "Are you saying that they are Donald Trump want-a-bees, at least when it comes to wealth?"

"It is likely, although with better hair."

"What do most Muslim's want?"

"Living in Luxor and having had discussions with people from every part of the world, I have come to believe that we, consistent with a single community, want much the same things—To feel safe, have life be predictable and not chaotic, feel closeness to others, and be free of poverty. Maybe even those with radical beliefs, or at least the typical supporter, see their way as providing these things. Many people have lost the sense of community, and some appear to seek it in these radical organizations."

"You think that they feel threatened?"

"The word "jihad" is spoken suggesting that there is oppression, but as I mentioned those at the top probably have more personal wealth and power motives, and create the impression of oppression. That said, many Muslims in our area of the world do feel that the Western capitalist system doesn't work in their favor."

"I've heard that word, "jihad" many times but what does it mean?"

"Probably not what you are thinking it does. "Jihad" comes from the Arabic word jahada, and means "he made an effort." It is very important to make an effort in the cause of God, but this is usually personal betterment and achievement, which is one reason why Muslim scholars have been so influential in disciplines like mathematics and astronomy. For example, algebra and algorithms were invented by Muslim scholars. To defend Muslim's against persecution is another jihad, although Mohammed considered fighting a lesser jihad. So, if those associated with terrorism see that they are being persecuted, then a jihad applies, but if conquest only is the goal, jihad does not apply."

"Why is it so important to make an effort?"

"The Qur'an indicates that people can go to heaven or hell, depending on the balance of good and bad deeds during their life. There is said to be a Last Day or Day of Judgment, when the world will be destroyed and Allah will raise all people from the dead to be judged. Those with mainly bad deeds will go to hell and suffer spiritual and physical torment, while those with mostly good deeds will go to heaven to experience spiritual and physical pleasure. Until this day deceased souls remain in their graves, but they have a sense of their destiny."

"That's quite the motivation to do good in life and make an effort! What are heaven and hell said to be like?"

"Heaven or paradise is also known as "The Garden" with lofty mansions, delicious food and drink, and virgin companions, and has seven levels depending on your achievements in this life. Like heaven, hell has seven levels with the lowest a cauldron of boiling liquid, and the degree of offense determines the level. The path to heaven is described as a bridge over hell, and those weighed down by their bad deeds will fall in, I suppose limiting the need for a full judgement by God."

Catching what would seem to be an inconsistency, I interjected, "If a person kills in battle, or by committing a terrorist attack, doesn't that deed condemn them to hell?"

"Ah, the Qur'an grants a couple of automatic exceptions, the first being that warriors who die fighting in the cause of God are ushered immediately into God's presence, and second, so-called "enemies of Islam" are sentenced to hell upon their death."

"Does that mean that I, not being a Muslim, am automatically sentenced to hell?" It sounds incredibly harsh, and on the flip-side very lenient for warriors of Islam.

"Do you hate Muslim's and fight against Islam?"

"No, of course not!"

"Then you have nothing to fear, but you see how interpretation can justify extreme beliefs. Some might say that if you are not Islamic you are an enemy and so sentenced to hell. Also, that if persecution is a justification for a jihad, the warrior goes right to God and paradise, not having to wait in a grave until the Day of Judgement."

"Yes, I see things more clearly now. The virgin companions must be quite the side-benefit."

Smiling Ahmed winked, "Or the main one."

To say the least Ahmed's insights greatly impressed and even inspired me. From our short conversation, my Western influenced perspective on Islam has shifted, dare I say, radically. I see how appealing Islam must have been to potential converts during its early years, leading now to something in the order of one-quarter of the world's population considering themselves to be Muslim. If nothing else dispensing with all the confusion over multiple Gods was a major draw. Islam represents purity of belief and life, and a simplicity of faith. Not wanting to take too much more of Ahmed's time I thanked him for the tour and information, leaving a little donation for the mosque.

Although I learned a great deal from Ahmed, I want to acquire more information, but where to go from Egypt? Mecca and Medina would be great, but Saudi Arabia, and certainly the main Islamic sites there, are closed to most Westerners. Surfing the Internet in the hotel I transferred to from the Nile boat, I happened upon a photo of the Blue Mosque in Istanbul. "Now that's a site to visit!" popped out effortlessly. Turkey is a destination on my "bucket list," although maybe it's too early in life for such a list. Sealing the deal, I read that Turkey was at one point the center of Islamic power, and more importantly flights from Cairo are really affordable.

Staring up at the several towering minarets on the Sultan Ahmed Mosque, or Blue Mosque, in Istanbul, I recalled my pleasure at seeing the minaret in Luxor. These ones, though, are fit for a king, or sultan as it turns out. I wonder if the Sultan was a distant relative of Ahmed in Luxor. During my Internet searches, I learned that Muslim's tend to go by fewer names than do those of Christian and Jewish faiths, so it's unlikely that his background includes supreme power in Turkey. Consistent with such supreme power the mosque is almost overwhelming, with six minarets, and from what I can make out from my vantage point, five major domes and several smaller ones.

Wanting to learn as much accurate information as possible I decided to join a tour group. Our elderly guide seemed to want to talk more than walk. Due to the excess detail of the presentation, I only absorbed what seemed to be the key bits and pieces. Apparently, Sultan Ahmed had the mosque built to assert, or reassert, Ottoman power following a resounding defeat in the 1603-1618 war with Persia. However, given that they lost, the mosque could not be built using wealth confiscated during the war, as was the tradition, and hence it came from the Treasury. Naturally, there were those who resented this cost, and he earned some enemies in the process. I'd really never thought of war as a funding strategy for improvement projects, but there you have it. Of course, if the war doesn't go as planned the politician ends up with the cost of war, and the cost of improvement projects.

Based upon what I'm hearing and seeing the cost of the mosque must have been as enormous as the mosque itself is physically. The architect, Sedefkar Mehmed Aga, combined

Byzantine, Christian (of the nearby Hagia Sophia), and traditional Islam styles to design this most impressive structure. Matching the grandeur of the exterior, the interior has more than 20,000 handmade tiles with over 50 unique tulip designs. The Sultan fixed the price to be paid for each tile, but since the cost of each tile rose, doesn't that sound familiar, the quality of the tiles decreased as construction progressed. In our modern society, there just ends up being cost overruns, but since the Sultan Ahmed was already making enemies by taking from the treasury instead of the spoils of war, I guess he had to be careful.

Eventually moving from the exterior to the interior, we got to see some of what our guide has been talking about. The prayer area brings to mind the mosque in Luxor with the open space, although many times larger. The domed ceiling lets in enough light to illuminate the interior through 200 stained glass windows. However, to improve illumination circular rows of lights hang down, where ostrich eggs used to be placed to discourage spiders, and the webs they would invariably weave. Given all the cost associated with the 20,000 ceramic tiles, not to mention the labor installing them, light is important. Our guide explained that the upper section was painted blue, likely because the Sultan was running low on cash.

Although the size of the interior produces a sense of power and simplicity, it could sway to more of a cave-like feeling, if not for the colorful walls, stained glass windows, and also carpets with striking symmetrical designs. The central feature of the interior, although not in the center, is the mihrab, a semicircular niche in the wall closest to Mecca, that Muslims face while praying. This one is crafted from marble, capped by a dome, with columns to the sides. To the right of it is the minbar, not to be confused with minibar, a pulpit where the imam stands while delivering the sermon. Text from the Qur'an on blue tiles and stained glass compliments this crucial part of the mosque.

As it turns out, our tour of the Blue Mosque is drawing to a close, because the midday prayer time approaches, and the mosque is closed to non-Muslims during prayer time. Our aging guide by talking and not walking has limited our experience of the interior, but given the simplicity of design, there is not that much else to see, or at least that's what he claims. Maybe being aware of this reality he deliberately limited our exposure to it. On the way out, of course walking slowly, I examined the tiles, noting the detail and how the natural symbols portrayed, such as tulips, also characterize many of the Egyptian drawings. While anything but natural, the mosque being a miracle of architecture, there is that connection to nature, such as with the tulips and the natural light. We seem to have lost much of this connection moving forward in time.

Shortly after departing the mosque, the loud speakers on it blasted out the Islamic call to worship. From readings, I learned that five prayer times are required—before sunset, midday, afternoon, sunset, and night—with the exact times determined by the position of the sun. I wondered how this would work in the Arctic, with stretches of no sun in the winter and all sun in the summer. Clearly, they hadn't planned on many Inuit followers. However, from what I learned from Muslim friends in medical school, not all Muslims adhere to the prayer requirement, and more liberal interpretations hold that you try the best you can. I recall one Muslim medical student who was so devote that he at times left teaching sessions to prepare for prayer and engage. Maybe not surprisingly, he failed out of medical school. Even though this type of experience could foster resentment against Western ways, he held no anger towards the system, probably because his true faith sustained him so well.

Before exiting the grounds of the Blue Mosque, I turned to take a last look, once again marveling at the minarets and domes. The arrangement of the minarets appears to create a path for worshippers as they approach, or that's the sense I have. The destination clearly being the large dome standing above the smaller ones, that I had recently stood below.

Smiling at the experience, and also the thought of our guide not even making it into the interior if he still had the job 10 years from now, I turned without paying attention to those around me, resulting in my arm striking a strikingly beautiful young woman, wearing a hijab covering her hair, but not face. Seeing my look of shock, she smiled but rapidly changed her expression as the stern looking man next to her looked our way. I apologized and walked away. From my Internet readings, I learned that the Qur'an does not say that women have to cover their head or face, but just dress modestly, traditionally interpreted as covering their breasts and genitals. However, with so many things this proscription has been interpreted in other ways, many believing that modestly involves covering the hair, and still others that the whole face except the eyes need be hidden from male viewing, aside from male relatives by birth or marriage. I read that Saudi Arabia back in the earlier part of the 20th century was more liberal, but pressure from certain sects led the Royal Family to fear an uprising, and so they began to impose greater restrictions to the point where women have to cover up.

Most people feel sorry for Muslim women subjected to these restrictions, but I've heard that most are fine with it, and some even take advantage of the situation. During my training days, I met a male resident in surgery from Libya, who as chief resident in his home country, tried to get female residents and interns to do evening call, but they complained that it was against Islamic doctrine to have them out at night without a male relative. He replied something to the effect of "Nice try!" but had a battle on his hands. Of course, the society he was part of allowed women to work as doctors, or work at all, in contrast to some Muslim countries and regions. I'm sure that some prefer it this way, though, as work is tough. I wonder how many men would take advantage of a religious rule that gave them a way out of work. I suspect it would be many.

Walking along the busy street I tried to sort out my next move. So far, I have acquired quite a bit of information about Islam, but feel I need to learn more before moving on from the first of the Big 3 monotheistic religions, that was actually the last to arise. What I need is someone who can give me a picture of what Islam means to the average Muslim. Suddenly it came to me that a doctor friend back in British Columbia once spoke of a Muslim friend of his, an ophthalmologist, practicing in Istanbul. I texted my friend in Canada and before finishing a cup of Turkish coffee in a quaint coffee shop, I had the ophthalmologist's name and contact information. Calling instead of texting I encountered a recording in a language I did not recognize, but left a detailed message explaining my reason for calling. Muhammed, the name clearly confirming his Muslim identity, calling a few hours later near dinner time when I was back at my hotel. He agreed to meet with me that night at a coffee shop he gave the address to.

Compared to my casual clothing consisting of jeans, a polo shirt, and running shoes, Muhammed is over-dressed, or I under-dressed, his attire consisting of crisp black leather shoes polished to a luster such that they reflect light, black dress pants, and a royal blue dress shirt buttoned down at the neck. Fortunately, he had not bothered with a tie. Hoping that I am not insulting him by dressing so casual I took a look around the coffee shop, and noticed that if anything I am over-dressed for the establishment. Still I decided to apologize after the introductions, "I regret not dressing better."

"Oh, don't concern yourself with that, I just came from my clinic. If this was a surgery day you might be over-dressed compared to me." He chuckled at the last statement.

I found myself instantly warming up to Muhammed, and imagined his patients liking him. After explaining my reason for visiting Turkey and request that we meet, he leaned back and folded his hands behind his head.

"Most people who visit here want to see the ancient architectural sites, so your reason is unique. I'll certainly try and help, but please appreciate that no one would put me forward as a scholar of Islam, although I am well read and have practiced since childhood."

"That's the type of information I'm looking for. Not some sterilized version but the real take on it."

"Well then fire away, but let's first order some coffee."

Our coffees and pastries arrived seemingly minutes after ordering them, with only casual conversation about the weather and Istanbul during this interval. The brief break gave me a chance to consider how I want to start. A direct approach is likely best. "What has Islam meant for you?"

"Wow, that's quite the starter. Thank God, or I should say Allah, for this coffee and sugar loaded pastries." Smiling he continued, "My parents were observant but not obsessive with it, so we prayed 5 times a day if feasible, but I have to admit I went to fewer times per day while I was in medical school and residency. I think for me it was more the motivation to better myself and learn. This is something my parents emphasized as core to their beliefs. It is a true jihad, and not this stuff you hear about in the western world."

"You've obviously achieved that, so I'm sure your parents are pleased."

"Yes, they are very pleased at my success, but would have been fine with less so long as I made an effort."

"What else is desired or expected?"

"There are 5 pillars of Islam serving as guides to how Muslim's might best live. The first is the notion that as quoted,

"There is no god but God, and Mohammed is the messenger of God." I'm sure you've encountered that one." After I nodded in the affirmative he continued, "The second is Salat, or the five prayers a day, that I often convert to a few, in the direction of the Ka'ba in Mecca. Third is the Sawn, meaning daily fast performed throughout the month of Ramadan, where we refrain from food, drink, and sexual intimacy during daylight hours. I can't say I've been completely adherent to any of those but I try. The idea here is to have discipline and experience the suffering of the poor. The Festival of Breaking the Fast ends Ramadan, and involves prayers and the exchanging of gifts. We all tend to like this more than the fast. The fourth pillar is often done at the end of Ramadan, as it fits, namely giving to the poor or charitable causes, about one-fortieth of a person's wealth. The fifth and final pillar is Hajj meaning a pilgrimage to Mecca and the Ka'ba in the 12th Islamic month, at least once. Islam goes by the lunar calendar. You might have noticed the crescent moon symbol."

"Yes, I did, and wondered why the moon was so featured, unlike with the ancient Egyptians who worshipped the sun."

"Well that's the reason."

"Have you made the pilgrimage to Mecca?"

"No not yet, but I'll get there someday, it will happen." Muhammed seems like he is motivating himself with that last statement, a bit of guilt induction.

"That black structure is so mysterious looking, and the image of people circling it striking. What's the significance?"

"The Ka'ba is ancient and believed by many to have been where Adam, the first man supposedly, founded a sanctuary. Even if this is not the case, it was an early shrine to numerous Arabian deities. Muslim's believe that God commanded Abraham and his son, Ishmael, to build the Ka'ba on the site of the ancient shrine. Mohammed rededicated the shrine to the one true God."

"From what I've learned so far this is a key theme with many Gods worshipped earlier on, and then a shift to a single God."

"Yes, I guess that's true, and Islam epitomizes the single God model."

"I recall from pictures that there are designs on the Ka'ba. What do they stand for?"

"They are words woven in cloth from what I've heard, although I can't say yet from personal experience, that largely cleanse the shrine of polytheism, and transform it into a shrine to God."

"So, the shift from many to one is embodied in the inscriptions?"

"It seems so."

Deciding to shift the focus slightly I raised a point that is puzzling me. "I keep hearing terms for Muslims like Sunni, Shia, Sufis, and even more since coming to Turkey. What do they mean?"

"Sunni, which I am and most Turkish Muslims are, follow the Sunna, or customary practice of Mohammed, based on six collections. I'm not totally clear on what all the other Muslim sects stand for, but one thing that's clear is what we lack in polytheism we more than make up for in diversity of belief systems within Islam. Not only major divisions but subdivisions within these, and in some cases subdivisions within the subdivisions, that I can't even follow, nor try to. The most colorful of the major categories, though, is Sufism that is here and in Egypt. Sufis seek a close and personal experience of God, and they have devised some interesting ways to facilitate that closeness. Take the Mawlawiyya order here in Turkey with their whirling dervishes, where they dance so intensely that they dissociate from their own being and commune with God."

"I can see how that would run against the grain of other Muslims opposing movie, dance and the like."

"Yes, the divisions within are in many ways as great or greater than those between Islam, Christianity, and Judaism, although don't tell anyone I said that."

"I'm beginning to see that the "monotheistic Big 3" are really cut from the same cloth, and one very distinct from polytheism."

"I suppose you're right, but both forms provide followers with a meaning to life, and also hope for an afterlife. You know, if you keep up with your information gathering you might end up teaching this religious stuff, and then I'll be buying you a coffee and pastries."

"Speaking of this "religious stuff" I think I'm going to visit Israel next to see what I can learn about the Jewish faith."

"That's a good place for monotheistic religion for sure, and its origins."

I spent the next hour or so conversing with Muhammed about medical practice in Turkey, and left impressed by the high standard of education and care. It pleases me to add him to my list of friends, or at least contacts, although I think that we would make good friends if I was to stay around. People toss that term around too lightly, with casual contacts on Facebook, being friends. I tend to reserve it for those I resonate with in actual conversation, and special friends those I can call upon for assistance. It seems that Muhammed would fit into the latter category given how he met with a stranger so fast, and is so helpful by nature. With a bit of luck my journeys to come will yield more friends, and not just contacts. Before leaving Turkey, I visited the standard tourist sites on a package tour, since it would be silly to leave and not see them. During these excursions, I kept thinking about how Israel might satisfy my curiosity, given the role that the geographic region played and still plays in the monotheistic Big 3.

JUDAISM

A couple of hours was all it took to fly from Istanbul to Jerusalem. I thought of how much longer this journey would have taken in ancient times, and the experiences, good and bad, along the way. The only experience I'm having is the sense of being compressed with the lack of leg room. I recall reading an article about how flying might worsen circulation in the body. Not surprising when your legs are being squeezed into a far too small space. Taking a bus might have been better, but after "the horror" I try to minimize bus travel. Modern day flights, though, have largely degraded into flying buses, and not even the luxury version, but flying school buses. The train was another option, but the cost is about the same and travel time much greater. Hence, I opted for the flying discount bus.

A medical school friend, David, who is now conducting research at the Hebrew University, agreed to meet me at the airport. While in medical school he also did a PhD in immunology, and discovered more funding opportunities in Israel where his parents were born. When I contacted him about meeting up he was very excited, and even more so when I mentioned my interest in Judaism. He feigned disappointment when I indicated my intent is not to convert.

Now standing in front of me he exclaimed, "You'll be staying with me for a few days." Winking he added, "Maybe we'll see about your conversion."

"Staying with you?" I had asked him to book me into a hotel of his choosing. "I never intended for you to put me up."

"Well this way you'll save money and have a more authentic experience. My research affords some flexibility, so I've taken a couple of days off to show you the sites."

"Thanks, your generosity is really appreciated!"

"I have to say that I don't recall you being all that interested in religion, and certainly Judaism. Is the interest related to that amazing brush with death?"

Even though I had not told him, it seems that the world, or at least the part I'm connected to, has heard about it. "Yes, it got me wondering about the bigger picture. I didn't mention it when I called though, so how'd you hear about it?"

"I keep up with the news from North America, and it was all over. Besides, many of those from our medical school class have been passing information back and forth about it. Surely you must have been contacted by some."

"Yes, by quite a few." I neglected to mention that it was tiring to keep going over the details. "Why didn't you mention it when I contacted you?"

"Why didn't you bring it up?"

"To be honest I'm kind of tired talking about it."

"So I figured, and thought I'd wait for the opportunity to raise it, and that chance just happened."

"Admittedly, the whole experience peeked my curiosity in the bigger picture of life and death."

"I'd be surprised if it didn't, and with any luck you might discover an answer here. If there is an answer to be found in religion, you've certainly come to the right place. Jerusalem is ground zero for some of the major religions. It can be quite confusing, but I'll try and help bring it together for you. First, let's go back to my place, get you settled, and then go out for a dinner where I'll go over some of the background information."

The restaurant selected by my friend was busy and had an aura of warmth about it, despite the fairly plain interior. It might have been the wood tables and chairs that contributed to the atmosphere, or maybe just the energy of the people.

After ordering some wine and appetizers David launched into almost a presentation. "I've been considering how best to present Judaism and think I'll start in the present." Catching my puzzled look, he quickly added, "In some ways the present relates to the beginning, that's why. We are now sitting in what was once known as Canaan, the center of the world, because it lay between Egypt to the south, Mesopotamia to the east, and the Hittites to the north. Traders went back and forth along this corridor of sorts, where my ancestors lived. It is believed that we descended from Abraham, who was supposedly a wandering Aramaean, although I don't recall who these people were."

Catching on I added, "So this is really the home of the Jews."

"Exactly, or at least how we see it. Others often disagree."

"That's shocking, people disagreeing about territory."

Smiling at my dark humor David continued, "Abraham was the first Jew, and his life and wanderings are recounted in the book of Genesis. God is said to have made an agreement with Abraham that he would be the father of a great nation. Unfortunately, Abraham was not producing any children, although God repeatedly promised him that his descendants would be as numerous as the stars of heaven, as the sand on the shore, and the dust of the Earth."

"That's a lot of pressure!"

"To say the least, and Viagra wasn't yet invented."

While David laughed at his own humor a realization came to mind. "So, is that why the Jewish people consider themselves the chosen people?"

"Yes, because God made the agreement with Abraham and his descendants, although the latter part got off to a rocky, or perhaps soft, start."

Laughing with him I commented, "Ah, our talk is bringing back all that good medical humor."

"Don't you love it?"

"You know I do. Beyond the fun, it certainly helped us cope in medical school, and can take the heaviness off religion."

"Here's another interesting aspect to the story—When Abraham still failed to have children God established a sign, namely that "every male among you shall be circumcised," and all Jewish boys are circumcised when eight days old to symbolize the agreement between God and Abraham."

"What you're saying is that if Abraham was more, shall I say "robust," Jewish males would not have to be circumcised?"

"We'll never know, but possibly."

"Of course, he must have succeeded given that the Jewish race wasn't restricted to one person."

"The story gets still more interesting, because it was only at 86 that Abraham had a child with his wife Sarah's servant, Hagar. The child, Ismael, though was not a legitimate heir, and Hagar and

Ishmael were cast out. God protected them and Ishmael grew up to father a people, the Ishmaelites identified with the Arabs."

"Wow, this is better than keeping up with the Kardashians!"

"You see how drama is so part of human nature, and the historical drama continues because Abraham eventually had a child, Isaac, with Sarah, and as a final test of obedience God instructed Abraham to sacrifice Isaac. Abraham built a fire and tied up the boy, but God then told him to spare the child seeing that his obedience was so strong."

"Maybe we should keep the child and fire bit from the Kardashians."

"It will boost their ratings even higher though."

"True, and even though we probably shouldn't be linking the Kardashians to your history, drama and storytelling is a common link."

"There's more drama to come in the origins of my people, actually much more but I'll limit it. Jacob, Abraham's grandson, was quite the character, tricking blind and dying Isaac, his father, into blessing him with his older brother's birthright. Escaping from his brother he had a vision of a ladder, Jacob's ladder, with angels on it. God spoke to Jacob saying that the land he lay on would be given to him and his descendants forever. Later when he returned to submit to his brother he again met with God, and seemed to be wrestling with a stranger all night. At dawn the stranger told him that his name was now Israel because he had striven with both God and men, and prevailed."

"Not to put down your religion, but it seems that there were a quite a few visions and unusual sensory experiences in that family, and you know what psychiatrists would call that."

"I've read that hallucinations are actually quite common in the population, and do not indicate schizophrenia. Many early figures in our, and also Islamic and Christian history, had these experiences in the desert, and often at night. You can kind of see how that environment would be conducive to them. A psychiatrist might say they were only self-generated, but much more was ascribed to them at the time, yielding a whole religion, or perhaps I should say three religions."

At this point in the discussion our dinner arrived, providing a natural break in the conversation. The information is fascinating but there's a lot to absorb. I never really understood how the Jewish people originated, and why they are so strong in their conviction that this region is their homeland, but it's now coming into focus. Recalling how Muhammed had also heard the word of God but had it recorded exactly to produce the Qur'an, I thought of the Jewish book, the Torah. "Your description, aside from being entertaining, is really informative, but one thing you haven't mentioned is the big book. Didn't Abraham produce the Torah?"

"I appreciate your feedback on my storytelling, I've never considered myself to be that good at it." Pausing momentarily to collect his thoughts he continued, "The Torah is another major part and I'll give you the story on that as best I can. The Torah is often translated as "the law" but it's really instruction or guidance. The first five books of the bible contain the Torah, providing 613 commandments that are crucial to Jews."

"613! My God (yes, a slip of tongue) that's a lot of things to remember to do or not to do."

"And that's why there's the Ten Commandments amounting to the most important. Can you imagine if there were the "613 Commandments" instead of ten?"

"That would require quite the memory capacity."

"Most of the 613 are rituals, rules of hygiene, and moral laws, important but not the Big 10. Moses in the 14th century before Christ led the Israelites out of the slavery they were subjected to in Egypt, camping in the wilderness of the Sinai Peninsula. At night Moses climbed the mountain, reportedly with thunder, lightning, and smoke. With Joshua as a witness God spoke to Moses and gave him stone tablets containing the Ten Commandments. Think what it would have been like with all 613 commandments!"

"Yes indeed, 613 would not be so believable. Remind me what the Ten Commandments are?"

"Ah, I feel like back in Hebrew school being asked things like this. The first two state that Jews must worship the one true God, and that the real God is too overwhelming to be contained within an image. The third is that God is too great for his name to be taken in vain. We don't say his name at all, but speak of the Lord, although for our talks I'll say God. The fourth is Jews must keep the Sabbath holy, much as God did on his seventh day of creation. The fifth commandment is that children should honor their parents, and not just if the parents purchase video games and the like for them. Okay, I added that last part, but this commandment seems quite neglected. The sixth is "Thou shall not kill," another that is highly ignored, at least when we consider wars. The seventh forbids adultery, only referring to extramarital relationships and not premarital sex. Another one that is neglected. The eighth is "Thou shall not steal," I guess somewhat better adhered to, although not by everyone. The ninth is not to give false testimony against your neighbor, and the tenth is to avoid covetousness, like to covet a neighbor's wife."

"Most of them appear designed to improve social stability."

"Definitely. Pretty good rules to go by, and have stood the test of time, other than for adherence to many of them."

"What about worship and prayer?" I had an image of the Islamic Call to Prayer and worship five times per day. "Does it have to be at set times."

"No, not like with Islam. A person can pray at any time or any place, but the morning, afternoon, and evening services in synagogues date back to early times with sacrifices. The term "synagogue" refers to congregation or assembly. It is said that through prayer all spiritual realities are revealed. A synagogue is to point in the direction of Jerusalem, like the Islamic orientation to Mecca. The rabbi is the leader and religious teacher, the cantor the leader of services, although liturgical, meaning public, services are often led by members of the congregation. There is supposed to be a minimum of ten men for a service to occur. The daily prayer book is known as the Siddur and the festival prayer book the Mahzor."

"I'm sure that women must like the ten men minimum."

"Despite Jewishness, if that's a word, passing through the woman, our religion and culture is quite male centered, a remnant from ancient times no doubt. This is one of the reasons for reform versions of Judaism, to give women a more prominent role."

"Yes, with Islam even though there is only one God there are numerous divisions from what I've learned."

"We have those divisions too. Early on our people were dispersed, with the Ashkenazim living mainly in central Europe and the Sephardim in Spain and the Mediterranean. Subdivisions of these have occurred, and various levels of devotion also. For instance, Hasidism arose in Eastern Europe, with the men wearing black coats, hats, and long beards, and the women dressing in somber colors with wigs when they go out. They are very devoted and often consider reform Jews, to be non-Jews. With orthodox and traditional Judaism, women and men are separated at services, like with Islam, and the men have the more prominent role. Reform dispenses with this division and favoritism, and women have actually been made rabbis! Quite a shift."

"The old in-group and out-group distinctions."

"Yes, but maybe due to the persecution we have experienced over time, we feel a solidarity despite the distinctions. Adversity often reinforces in-group values and beliefs. For example, we adhere to the same holidays and 354-day calendar. Passover commemorates the exodus of the Israelites from Egypt. Rosh Hashanah is our New Year and Yom Kippur is the Day of Atonement. The last one is interesting as in one day you can purge all your sins for the year and start fresh!"

"Wow, talk about a great opportunity. I wonder if swindlers like Bernie Madoff have tried that one in court as an alternative to jail?"

"Somehow, I don't think that it would wash, but it could make for an interesting argument." After a few seconds he added, "You know, at this point, particularly because we're finished our dinner, I suggest we take a break from the discussion, and resume tomorrow when I take you to the Old City. Then we can go over other key aspects of Judaism."

"Good idea as all this information is starting to be overwhelming, although I doubt it could be presented better."

In the hope of not having to share the sites with many people, we left David's flat early and took a brisk walk to the Old City. Although it only occupies about a square kilometer, the Old City is jammed packed with history, and as we discovered, tourists and worshippers even at this early hour. Entering the Jewish quarter, appropriate given my current focus, we immediately came upon a site I have seen many times in photos and videos—A stone wall with Jews bowing towards it, the famous Western Wall. An attendant handed both of us a kippa, the small Jewish skullcap, that we had to put on before proceeding.

Approaching the Western Wall, David exclaimed, "This is the most important site in Jewish culture! Do you know why though?"

Trying to recall my history I answered, "I know it was part of something larger at one time."

"Exactly, it was part of The Temple, and this is all that remains. Now you might wonder what "The Temple" was, and for that we need to go back into Jewish history. Our first prophet, Samuel, was told by God to appoint a king, but the one he chose, Saul, did not work out to God's liking so he appointed David, King David. Not a direct relative of mine though despite the similarity in names." He smiled at his own humor.

"David proved himself by rising to the challenge when the Philistine army arrived and their giant, Goliath, issued a challenge of personal combat with any soldier who dared confront him. David was the only contender, and felled Goliath with a single stone from his slingshot. King David made Jerusalem his capital and ruled from 1001 to 968 before Christ. Later on, King David's son, Solomon, built the Temple to hold the Ark of the Covenant, our key religious relic, constructed under Moses."

"I recall that from Raiders of the Lost Ark."

"Most people probably do, but I doubt that lightning emerges from it. Getting back to our story, which will now have to compete with Raiders of the Lost Ark." He feigned a look of disappointment before continuing, "The Temple was supposed to be amazing with a series of courtyards. From outer to inner, the first was one that non-Jews could enter, the Court of Gentiles, followed by the Court of Women, then the Court of Israelites for men only, and finally the Court of Priests. Quite the hierarchy built in. The Holy of Holies, was the central sanctuary where the Ark of the Covenant was kept, that only the High Priest could enter, and even then only on the Day of Atonement."

"So where did it all go?"

"It would be amazing if it was still present, but history tends to take away the good, which is why the Western Wall has been called the Wailing Wall, due to some Jews "wailing" at the loss. The Babylonians destroyed it in 586 before Christ, but it was rebuilt on a smaller scale shortly after, and then on a much grandeur scale by King Harod the Great in the first century before Christ. Finally, the Romans destroyed it 70 years after Christ, and this is all that's left."

"Why hasn't someone rebuilt it for Judaism, and as a tourist attraction?"

"You see how it's attached to that other structure?" When I nodded, he added, "That's Temple Mount, a platform from which the Jewish Temples were constructed. It also holds the Dome of the

Rock, admittedly a beautiful Islamic shrine, constructed in 691 after Christ, that is their third holiest shrine after Mecca and Medina. There is also the Al-Aqsa Mosque on the site. I doubt that even the most aggressive and successful developer in the world would succeed in getting the Islamic sites knocked down to make way for a rebuilt Jewish Temple."

"Yes, I can see how that would trigger some conflict."

"So we're left with a wall. Who knows, maybe the symbolism is greater than the reality, particularly given that some of the Temple structures might be viewed as outdated, with separate courtyards for men and women."

I thought of the Ka'ba in Mecca, initially a site for multiple ancient Gods and developed to symbolize their overthrow and the supremacy of one God. "Symbols can indeed be more powerful than reality." Smiling broadly, I added, "If the Temple was still here it would probably be surrounded and encased in a newly developed "Temple Condominiums" complex commanding a price fit for King David."

"I wouldn't be surprised."

Taking a stroll from the Western Wall we shortly arrived at a sign with the name Zion Gate.

Before I could ask David explained, "This connects the Old City to the area of Mount Zion where King David's tomb is located."

Thinking of King David in his tomb I became curious about the Jewish version of the afterlife. "What does Judaism have to say about life after death? Is there a heaven and hell?"

"Compared to Christian and Islamic faiths, Judaism doesn't emphasize the afterlife, but we do cover it. I suspect that every religion does, or it might just be called history instead of religion."

"Good point. Why does Judaism deemphasize it though?"

"There's no definite answer, but one possibility is that Israelites were slaves in Egypt, and Egyptians were obsessed with the afterlife, as I'm sure you discovered. With the Exodus from Egypt it's possible that they wanted to distance themselves practically and conceptually from the Egyptians. Consequently, the first bibles making up the Torah had little to say about the afterlife."

"But it came later?"

"Yes, starting I believe with the Talmud, another of our great books, this one from the 6th century after Christ. Then there is the

Zohar by Rabbi Moses de Leon in the 13th century, purporting to reveal ancient wisdom. The book presents how God created the world via 10 sefrots or attributes. These are portrayed as a tree or candlestick, with severity and mercy divisions balanced on equilibrium. By acting in accordance with God's attributes a person's soul will achieve union with God."

"But what about heaven and hell?"

"In this regard, there is some variability as well, and even humor. For example, one version I heard is that heaven and hell depend on the strength of a person's religious beliefs, because Moses teaches the Torah all day long in the afterlife, and if you are very devoted this is heaven, but if not it is hell."

"That certainly simplifies it."

"Yes, but that is only one minor version, maybe by a standup comedian. There is said to be a heaven and hell. Heaven or Gan Eden, meaning the Garden of Eden is a place of peace and great joy, with banquets, sunshine, and sex."

"Sort of like an all-inclusive vacation to the Red Sea or Caribbean."

"Pretty much, but others emphasis the spiritual over the material, indicating that heaven is a place for worship and not anything of the flesh."

"What about hell, even though just worship all day could qualify?"

"Hell called Genion is where suffering occurs for up to a year, at which point the person either goes to the Garden of Eden, or if not purified is annihilated. This one-year time frame is the basis for families mourning the deceased and asking blessings over eleven months, to help ensure that he or she makes it out of Genion."

"If they haven't made it out by eleven months they probably won't by twelve."

"No, they're dust in the wind at that point. There is another aspect of the afterlife or what ties into it, that being the Messianic age. When our people were scattered from this region the belief arose that God will provide another king like King David, and that this king will make a covenant with the righteous and kill the wicked. At this point history will end and God's kingdom will be established on Earth. The righteous dead will then be resurrected."

"Do Jewish people really still believe that?"

"Many do and are hopeful that it will occur. For others, the creation of Israel is the dream realized. Jerusalem is known to our people as the City of David. In the late 1800's a Viennese journalist—Theodore Herzl—advocated for a Jewish state, and mentioned Palestine as the obvious location. He is said to be the founder of modern Zionism. Following the atrocities of World War II with the Holocaust, the creation of Israel became a reality. At first Jerusalem was partitioned, but came under our rule in 1967, and made into the capital of the Jewish world. Not exactly the end of history by God, maybe more the start for us in a sense, but overall a pretty good result."

"I'd say so, and interesting how Hitler's whole strategy actually backfired helping to advance the Jewish dream."

"Yes, the ironies of life. We started off yesterday talking about how the Jerusalem we find ourselves in now is the home of my ancestors, and have come around to the modern state of Israel, full circle."

Following a visit to King David's tomb we strolled back to the modern section of Jerusalem and had a late lunch. Instead of seeking more information about Judaism, as I felt I had absorbed about all I could, I raised another related topic. "It's interesting how Judaism and Islam share features, like the belief that God will return and destroy the existing world to usher in a new era for the believers, rules of conduct, and the notion of heaven and hell as possible destinations in the afterlife."

"Yes, and of course the single God model, that aligns with the power to end the existing world and start a new era."

"One question I have though is why Judaism did not spread like the Islamic religion? I've read that there are only about 14 million Jewish people making up .2% of the world's population, compared to around 1.6 billion for Islam, comprising approximately a quarter of the people on the planet."

"What about Christians?"

"I read an estimated 2.2 billion or a third of the population."

"Wow, I guess we really are a minority."

"But why?"

"Well the Holocaust didn't help with our numbers, but it's more I think that we haven't been aggressive about converting people compared to the other two monotheistic religions." Pausing he added, "See I still haven't converted you. Jewishness is something that people identify with based on a common heritage linked to this region historically, or to diverse communities Jews have settled in."

"I can see that, and can't recall hearing of pressure to convert unless a person marries a Jewish person."

"There you go, and where we're going tomorrow is to explore sites of the third monotheistic religion—Christianity. We won't be seeing the Islamic sites in the area, because the Temple Mount ones are closed to tourists, and you've already explored Islam. As with Judaism, Christianity starts here."

CHRISTIANITY

Departing early once again to minimize crowds, we entered the Old City and navigated our way through narrow streets before arriving at a fairly small courtyard, clearly a tourist site based on the number of people with cameras.

David introduced our destination, "This my friend is where it all began for Christianity, the Church of the Holy Sepulchre."

Looking at the fairly small structure, I was somewhat underwhelmed. "You mean that this was the first church?"

"No, no, this is where Jesus of Nazareth was crucified and buried, sepulcher means crypt or grave. According to Christianity he was also resurrected here."

With the mention of this the weight of history descended on me—A structure so seemingly insignificant from the outside having such significance to so many people! Before I could think of something to say David explained,

"As a Jew I'm not really supposed to acknowledge Jesus, but many of us believe, as do Muslims, that he was an actual person, a prophet. However, where Christianity diverges is in the belief that Jesus is the son of God, or in other words he's not fully human."

"Yes, that's quite a difference."

"And the basis of Christianity, but I'm not the best person to give you the historical low-down. Instead, I bought a couple of tour passes so we can both learn something."

While I thanked him, and offered to pay, he located the passes on his phone. Declining my offer of money, he led the way across the courtyard and through a curved doorway, a second one next to it walled off. An attendant scanned the tickets and directed us over to the side to wait for our guide.

After about a 5-minute wait, a 30's something, well-tanned man dressed in khaki clothes approached and introduced himself as

Mark, our private guide. He explained, "I try and make the tours interesting. I don't know about you both, but I find history far more exciting when there's a meaning or story, not just dates and facts."

Speaking for both of us I commented, "We can appreciate that from medical school, and the little medical history we learned."

"Good then let's see what story there is." Smiling he began, "In the beginning when I was a young child." As we laughed he asked, "You didn't book this tour to hear about my life story?"

Always fast to respond David replied, "We'll book that tour for tomorrow."

"Okay then, even though this Christianity thing might be slightly less interesting we'll start." Taking a breath, he began, "The present builds on the past, but also introduces changes. Going back many years the Jews were in this region, and Jesus was a wandering Jewish teacher. We don't know much about his life prior to his teachings, because the New Testament focuses on this three year or so period. The Old Testament consists of the first bibles that comprise the Jewish Torah. As I'm sure both of you have heard, Mary and Joseph were his parents, but the conception is described as immaculate, given that God, and not Joseph, is the father."

Feeling the need to comment I ventured, "From a medical perspective that leaves room for debate, although I recall a couple of teenage girls claiming it while their parents looked on." A story is one thing in my mind, but it has to be somewhat believable.

Nodding in understanding, Mark responded, "Christianity is expressed and can largely be understood in terms of parables, or simple story lines to illustrate a point, and the point here being that Jesus is the son of God, as opposed to a fully human prophet who hears the word of God. Jesus is both human, from Mary, and God-like from God, a nice blend of down-to-earth and other worldly. Another parable is that of the Sower, God's word being like seeds scattered by a sower, that sometimes fall on good ground and flourish, and at others falls on hard and stony ground where they do not flourish."

"So Jesus realized the value of these story-lines for getting the message out?" David had never appreciated this aspect before. "He must have anticipated the modern media age."

"Yes exactly, and he was indeed a good teacher. I also suspect that he learned the value of keeping it simple and understandable as he practiced his craft. Speaking of modern media, look at where we're at now with Twitter messages as simple as possible. Who knows, maybe he was God in part with that early insight." Realizing he was showing too much skepticism he added, "I don't mean to be disrespectful, but I sense you two aren't staunch adherents that will be offended, you're more trying to understand."

"I'm Jewish, and my friend here is trying to gain some insight into the bigger picture, already learning about the other monotheistic religions. I'm also curious, and wish to learn more about Christianity."

"Awe that makes sense, and curiosity is a really good thing. I'm sure that Jesus was also curious trying to see what would make a better world."

Having gained an insight from my excursion into religion, I raised a crucial point. "From what information I've encountered so far, people generate different stories, a given one not sitting with everyone. Ancient Egyptians created various Gods to suit their needs, and then there are divisions within the monotheistic Big 3, as I've come to call them, and then subdivisions within each of these."

"And Jesus introduced a very significant division that was not all that appealing to the Jewish powers at the time. Temple authorities strongly believed that the Messiah would bring God's kingdom on Earth, and Jesus was saying that a covenant with God depends simply on faith, and a life expressing that faith. Even more disturbing to the Temple authorities, he claimed that he spoke with God's authority and was restoring God's power to the world! Then when he refused to submit to the High Priest, an offense carrying the death penalty, he was handed over to the Roman authorities as a threat to the state."

"Politics rearing its ugly head again." I couldn't resist the comment.

"With a very tragic, but to Christians, also positive outcome."

Mark took us up a stairway. "This is the Calvary where Jesus was crucified. It's known as the Chapel of the Crucifixion." Pointing to an elaborate gold alter he continued, "The rocky wall or outcropping is really the alter, because Jesus was crucified there. Below the man-made alter is a hole where it's believed that the cross holding him was placed. Glass covers the rock on both sides." While examining it up close he explained, "Archeological investigations have shown that it was outside the city, but close enough to one of the gates, that it could well have been the crucifixion site." We watched as people knelt down to touch the ground by the alter.

Taking us back to the church entrance he pointed out a raised rectangular rock slab with knobs at the corners like bedposts, and a flat polished stone surface framed with marble. Lamps hang from a bar supported by 2 poles at the ends of the slab. I barely paid attention to it when standing waiting for Mark to arrive, as it did not seem particularly striking. "This is the Stone of Anointing where Jesus's body was prepared for burial." As we looked down a middle-age couple knelt before it, showing both great pleasure and pain in their expressions. Speaking quietly, Mark commented, "It can be a very profound emotional experience to devote Christians."

We took in the mural on the wall behind it, showing the Anointing on what more looked like a bed to me, and on the right side, a very striking image of what I interpreted to be Jesus being taken down from the cross. This visual backdrop really helped define the stone slab on the ground. "Quite the picture."

"Yes, a picture says more than words."

Thinking of other churches, I realized that this one is very different. Expressing my thought to Mark I mentioned, "This doesn't seem like an ordinary church."

"That's because it was largely built to house and protect these key Christian sites, instead of as a church per se. Several denominations have control, including Greek Orthodox, Armenian Orthodox, Roman Catholic, Egyptian Copts and others. Protestants and related denominations do not, as they arose later, I guess when territory had already been staked out."

"Who built it?"

"Initially a Roman emperor, Hadrian, in the second century after Christ's death, who built it as a temple to the goddess Aphrodite, mostly though to cover the cave where Jesus was buried. The Romans who ruled were not into monotheism as were the Jews and Christians. They still had their polytheistic beliefs, although over time many switched to the simpler single God belief system of Christianity."

Thinking of the combination of beliefs present in the region I commented, "I can see how there would be a great deal of tension and need for tolerance."

"Much as there still is in the region, and we all know how fragile that can be, although overall the Jews, Christians, and

Muslims seem to work it out to preserve the Old City religious sites."

An idea coming to mind David piped in, "Even with the differences they kind of form an in-group compared to polytheistic systems."

"That's probably true, but at the time of Jesus it seems that the Temple authorities did not see it that way, leading to his execution. Getting back to who built the church, the first Christian emperor, Constantine the Great, had a church built around 325 after Christ's passing. His mother is said to have discovered three crosses, and identified the one used to crucify Jesus by testing each on corpses. This special cross caused a corpse to rise whereas the others did not. She also discovered his grave, and the site where he was resurrected according to the story. We'll go to that site now."

While continuing on to it he explained, "The church has a long and colorful history, consisting of cycles of it being built up and then damaged, then built up. Various Muslim rulers led attacks against it, and in 1027 negotiations between the Islamic Fatimids and the Byzantine Empire resulted in it being rebuilt, with a courtyard open to the sky and 5 small chapels. It is believed that the First Crusade of 1099 was ordered by Pope Urban II, due to fears that the Church of the Holy Sepulchre would be destroyed as Fatimids and Turks fought over Jerusalem, or that might just have been a rationale. The Knights of the First Crusade took control of the area, and the crusade was actually viewed as an armed pilgrimage. Every crusader prayed here, at least those that survived the journey and battles. To cover the whole history of the church would take hours, and I know you're more interested in the religious aspect, but suffice it to say that the church has survived conflict, and even a fire in the 1800's. It might not be as large as some major churches, but it's one rugged little creation."

"Now we're going to see where Jesus was buried in a section of the church known as the Rotunda."

We shortly entered an open space beneath a multi-tiered dome, in a sense reminding me of the mosques I've seen given the openness. However, an oddly placed tall structure with columns, some holding lights, detracted from this impression. "What's that structure?"

Smiling Mark responded, "It does tend to get that reaction. This is the Aedicule or site of the Holy Sepulchre itself. An aedicule is a small shrine that gives significance to the contents, and the contents in this case are very significant."

Taking in the Aedicule from a distance I note a parapet running around the top, a picture of Jesus to the front, and what seems to be a small version of the Rotunda on the roof. It appears that the large Rotunda dome was built around the tomb. While I tried to imagine the burial itself Mark added,

"The story here, at least for Jesus, has four parts: The crucifixion, anointing, burial, and resurrection. Of course, we can't see evidence of the fourth, but the story goes that because Jesus said he would rise from the dead, Roman guards were placed by the tomb. He was buried on Friday and on Sunday morning he rose, an occurrence that if true, must have terrified the guards. Women from Galilee found the tomb empty, the location indicated by an angel. Jesus appeared to Mary Magdalene in a garden, proving he was Jesus by showing the crucifixion marks on his hands and feet. Christians believe that God entered the Church as the Holy Spirit fifty days after the Resurrection of Jesus."

"Wow, that's quite the story! The creativity is fascinating, even in this era of computer-based media." I thought it worth adding, "A person could be skeptical though of the rising from the dead part."

"Yes, but recall that Christianity can be understood in a sense as brief stories. What better story to affirm that Jesus is part God, then to have him do something that no one else can—Rise from the grave. If that doesn't convince you he's part God, then nothing will."

"Very true." I definitely get the story aspect, and how packaging the information in such a dramatic way has been so successful.

"Another fascinating aspect, or addition, to the story is that between his death and resurrection, Jesus went down to hell extending his work for God to people who could not have known him, given that they lived before his time."

"I've learned from my explorations so far that the heaven and hell aspect is shared by Christianity, Judaism, and Islam, although with slightly different takes on it."

"Yes, much is shared. Christians also believe that Adam and Eve were the first humans, and for disobeying God they were cast out of the Garden of Eden. Their sins are believed to affect all people, but Jesus substituted for people taking the punishment on the cross. However, it doesn't stop sinners from going to hell."

"In my religion, we have the Day of Atonement. Is there something like this in Christianity?"

"Judaism formalizes it more, but recall how the message Jesus presented was that a covenant with God depends only on faith and a life expressing that faith. Hence, even the worst criminal is redeemed by acquiring the faith, and also of course leading his or her life according to it."

Seeing another common theme, David added, "All three religions do provide motivation for doing good in life, despite temptations to do otherwise."

"People will be people though and drift to the bad, which is why I think these religions caught on, as a way of showing people the right course in life and motivating them to follow it, no matter how bad things are."

"And giving them hope for an afterlife." I felt that this aspect was being ignored by David and Mark.

"Both women and men are made part of the so-called living Body of Christ. Christians believe that the death of Jesus opens the way to eternal life for all."

"It seems that much of Christianity is focused on the death of Jesus. Why the emphasis on his death?"

"The ultimate punishment, at least in this life, for wrongdoings is death, capital punishment. For Jesus to pay for the sins of people he had to die, and not just of natural causes."

"I can see how a religion purporting that someone else will pay for your sins could catch on." The marketing value did not escape me.

"And particularly when that also buys you an eternal life! Furthermore, Christians like the ancient Greeks and Romans were quick to absorb cultural elements from regions that Christianity spread into."

Recalling the temples in Egypt built by the Greeks and Romans, I can see how this would advance Christianity. "Admission into Christianity must be quite simple then."

"Basically, it's just a matter of accepting Christ and living your life according to his teachings, although to formalize it a baptism is typically required. This involves water being sprinkled onto a person's forehead or immersion in water, to symbolize purification and admission. John the Baptist baptized Jesus at the start of his teachings. As Jesus raised himself from the water, heaven is said to have opened and the Holy Spirit descended on him like a dove."

"What does "living your life according to his teachings" actually mean?"

"Ah, good question and one that more people might want to consider, including many who consider themselves to be Christian. It refers to how a person treats others—If hungry give food, if thirsty give a drink, if a stranger make the person welcome, if lacking clothes dress the person, if sick help by visiting, and if in prison see the person. Later burying the dead was added, making up the seven works of mercy. On the other hand, the way not to live is characterized by the seven sins of pride, greed, lust, envy, gluttony, anger, and sloth, as these all place the individual above God and other people. By living according to the seven works of mercy you make it into heaven, while a life based on the seven sins, and hence neglecting the needs of others, guarantees you a place in hell!"

Considering the requirements for heaven and hell I had to comment, "Based on current realities, hell must be one busy place."

Laughing Mark replied, "Probably bursting at the seams. I heard from a little messenger that only a few people made it into heaven last year, but are on probation."

David piped in, "We certainly do live in an era of entitlement, everyone expecting everything and giving little or nothing to others. It's a valuable message, although perhaps somewhat black and white as life is often in the grey zone."

"Forgiveness is an aspect of Christianity, and these seven works of mercy and seven sins are another simple message, and one designed to oppose what people naturally seem to do—Place themselves as number 1, or even 1-to-10, thereby neglecting others."

"Even then, if this is at all true Jesus and God must be anguished by what they see, not to mention very lonely." I can only imagine how lonely.

"Christians believe in the Last Judgment by God, that some feel will come when the dead are resurrected and there is the second coming of Christ, while others feel it has already occurred."

"Let's hope it's the former, as if it's the latter we're toast!" Our discussion made me think of how self-serving people tend to be, and how far the modern world is from the ideal portrayed.

Switching the focus somewhat, Mark asked, "Speaking of toast do either of you know what symbolism bread has for Christianity?"

"The Last Supper." David responded with confidence.

"Yes exactly. Jesus went to Jerusalem for Passover with his disciples, knowing that death probably awaited him, given that the Temple authorities were very displeased with his teachings. He broke the bread and poured the wine, and told them to eat for the bread is my body, and drink for the wine is my blood of the covenant, poured out for many for the forgiveness of sins. In Christian services bread and wine symbolize the body and blood of Christ."

"Why is Jesus referred to as Christ?" I find the naming confusing, as he was really Jesus, but often referred to as "Christ."

Demonstrating his knowledge of Christianity once again, Mark easily answered, "Jesus is his name. Christ is the English translation of "Messiah," capturing how Jesus is the one chosen by God to save his people. In the Old Testament Messiah is used, and in the New Testament, Christ. When people say "Jesus Christ," they are using the word as his title—Jesus the Messiah—expressing his role, although many nowadays use it more in the context of expressing pain and anger, like when you hit your thumb with a hammer."

We had a good chuckle with Mark's insightful and all too true comment. He used the break to suggest, "Maybe it's time that we leave the church, unless you want to stay longer." Seeing that we were not opposed to leaving he continued, "We'll pass along the Via Dolorosa, translated as "Way of Grief" or "Way of Sorrow," the route Jesus took from prison to his crucifixion. However, we'll be going in the opposite direction to that taken by Jesus. I'll then take you to the Tomb of the Virgin Mary."

Exiting I was struck by the brightness, not realizing how truly dim the light was in much of the church. Placing my sunglasses on I walked in respectful silence noting the pilgrims tracing the last walk of Jesus. A sign on the rock wall listed the Via Dolorosa.

"The route we are on took Jesus from the Antonia Fortress, no longer present, to the crucifixion site, only 600 meters or about 2,000 feet, but the most important walk in history. Currently there are 9 Stations of the Cross, 5 in the church, but I believe there were

14 at one point." Walking the short but profound route in reverse, Mark pointed out the Ecce Homo Arch connecting two buildings, but almost obscured by other structures, with a couple of windows indicating at least one room. He also drew our attention to the exterior of the Polish Catholic Church, the 3rd station, with a carving in the stone face of the building depicting Jesus weighed down by the cross.

Leaving the Old City proper we walked to the Mount of Olives. Like with the Church of the Holy Sepulchre, I find the plain, almost white, stone facing of the entrance to the Tomb of the Virgin Mary to be somewhat underwhelming, particularly considering how significant Mary was and still is. As we stood looking at the fronting, I raised this point with Mark, "Maybe I'm thinking more of Roman Catholic grandeur, but the sites do seem subdued."

Supporting my perspective David expressed, "I'm thinking the same thing."

"It's all about understanding how things transpire, and the perspective that prevails at a given time. Early Christianity considered the so-called "Body of Christ" to mean numerous equal parts under one head. It was quite egalitarian. Roman Catholicism is very different. What part of "Roman Catholic" relates to the times they were in?"

"Roman!" Suddenly the significance came to me, never really thinking of why the term "Roman" is part of a Christian organization. "So, the Romans influenced it."

"Yes, partly because in the second century after Jesus many Romans converted to Christianity and were influencing Christian beliefs, and partly by the structure of their society impacting on Christian ways. Roman society, and even more so the army, was highly structured and hierarchical. Consequently, Christianity changed from egalitarian to hierarchical with a pope as the spiritual head of the church. Around 300 years after Christ's death and resurrection Christianity became the official religion of the Romans."

"Not everyone accepted this perspective though." Even with my limited, but growing, knowledge of religion I can think of other versions of Christianity, Protestantism being an obvious one.

"As with Islam and Judaism divisions emerged, such as Presbyterians and Congregationalists retaining the early egalitarian approach to the Body of Christ. Orthodox Christians, that now primarily consist of Greek and Russian Christianity, reject the notion of the pope having universal authority. This schism is often framed in terms of Eastern and Western Christianity, and of course the major fracturing of Western Christianity came with the Reformation in the 1500's producing Protestantism. The Roman Catholic Church, consistent with the authoritarian Roman structure, maintains that priests and the pope are the necessary intermediaries between Christ and people, leading to a great deal of corruption early on. Protestantism was largely a reaction to these problems, emphasizing that each person has a direct relationship with Christ. Then of course within Protestantism divisions occurred, such as Baptism, Lutheran, and Methodist."

Thinking of a humorous WKRP in Cincinnati rerun I watched, in which a minister tried to sell indulgences over the radio, I started to chuckle. Catching the questioning looks of Mark and David I stated, "Those indulgences the Roman Catholics had, whereby you could buy your way into heaven, must really have went over well with the poor masses in Europe. Can you imagine someone fulfilling most of the seven sins, and none of the seven works of mercy, buying a seat in heaven, and the poor schmuck with the reverse taking his place in hell!"

"Sort of like the 1%, or even fraction of 1%, of our population feeling entitled to everything, and probably seeing that they have a place reserved in heaven." David's perspective on this travesty aligning fully with my own, our shared views being one of the reasons we became such good friends.

Adding to the theme, Mark suggested, "Perhaps if the church sold positions in heaven to them for a substantial share of their wealth, we might have a way to redistribute money more evenly in a way consistent with the seven works of mercy."

"That's an idea, Mark, maybe you can float it amongst your friends and create a movement within Christianity."

"Maybe, but Christians hardly have a monopoly on greed."

"You got that right."

Walking into the tomb, Mark shifted the focus of our conversation, "It's funny how we're discussing greed at the Tomb of the Virgin Mary, who is recognized by people of different religions as a symbol of virtue. Women have fared better in Christianity than with the other two of your "monotheistic Big 3," and to a large extent that's due to Mary. It is recounted that Gabriel came to Mary, and through her faithful obedience she became the mother of Jesus."

"She brings to mind the notion of simple stories conveying Christianity." I feel I'm catching on to it all. "Mary represents all that is good and virtuous."

"Exactly, love and being humble, helping and the list goes on. All the good that a woman, or man for that matter, can aspire to is conveyed by Mary. Consistent with the seven acts of mercy, a truly Christian way of life is to assist others and convey love and caring."

An insight came to mind supporting the notion that I am indeed getting it. "When Jesus ascended to heaven and God after the resurrection, he was then leaving it up to people to carry the Holy Spirit forward on the planet!"

"Yes, I believe that's a key message of that part of the story. You're showing real insight into religion."

I found the perspective obtained to be very enlightening, and it replaced confusion over many aspects of Christianity with understanding. It really did involve getting the right perspective.

My thoughts were interrupted by Mark asking, "What do you think of the tomb?"

I expressed exactly what I felt, "Much more impressive than the outside, and it seems similar to much of what we saw at the Church of the Holy Sepulchre. That very old feel from the painting of religious scenes, and these ornate gold-colored chandeliers."

"They are of the same period and style." Pointing to a small opening in the alter Mark explained, "The actual tomb is in there. I'll wait here while you have a look."

Ducking our heads David and I entered the small enclosure, dominated by a raised whitish rock crypt with a glass cover. Half expecting to see something inside, the plain rock came as a surprise.

Exiting the near claustrophobic tomb, I raised this point with Mark, "I wasn't expecting a mummy, but at least something inside it, not just rock."

Smiling he replied, "I thought that's how you'd react. Mary reportedly was resurrected on the third day after her death. Her soul and body being taken to heaven and received by Jesus. Hence, we only see rock."

"A fitting end to our story with the mother of Jesus ascending as well."

"You're right. It does make a good ending, and speaking of endings, we've come to the conclusion of our tour. I'll give both of you my business card with email and website if you wish to contact me for further information, or book another tour." Smiling again he added, "Of course that tour of my early life could still be on for tomorrow."

Thanking him and giving a generous tip we left, slowly making our way back to a restaurant by David's flat.

Enjoying the Middle Eastern cuisine David asked, "So, since this pretty much wraps up your exploration of the monotheistic Big 3, what have you learned?"

"The short answer is "a lot" but at the same time there is no clear answer. Given that they are the "monotheistic Big 3" it's not surprising that there are similarities, and it's these points in common that stand out."

"Other than the single God belief what do you see that they share?"

"What stands out for me is the notion that people have a tendency to act in ways that are bad, and God via his prophets, or Jesus if you're Christian, can lead us to a better way. Those that follow the path of what is prescribed as being right end up in heaven, although it goes by different names and descriptions, and if bad end up in hell. This gives followers some meaning and structure to life and death. Each religion also holds that there is a judgment type day for all, and that the righteous will be taken to heaven if not already there. I guess that this judgment day has not yet occurred though."

"Interestingly, there is an offshoot of Judaism, called Messianic Judaism, believing that Jesus is the Messiah."

"Sort of merging Judaism and Christianity."

"Exactly, although it's not all that popular with either religion."

"Well, that's another thing I've learned: The only thing people agree on is not to agree. Look at the "Big 3" and then subdivisions within each of these. It's almost like man creates God, or describes God based on our desire to create new ideas and belief systems, or perhaps to just form in-group and out-group distinctions."

"Imagine in a thousand years, assuming that Judgment Day hasn't yet arrived, how many divisions there will be within each of these single God religions."

"Who knows, they might even return to multiple Gods to keep the distinctions going."

"You never know. Given that you've kind of run out of the single God systems, what's your next step, or perhaps I should ask, what multiple God system are you going to explore after this?"

"I'm returning to Canada to do another locum, and make some money to support my explorations. On the way back I think I'll stop in Europe and investigate the Greek and Roman belief systems."

"That makes sense given that the Romans had a major influence on this area."

"And the Greeks, as well as Romans, on my first stop, ancient Egypt."

"Well, good, or maybe I should say, God luck to you!"

ANCIENT GREEK RELIGION

It must have happened after clearing customs at Athens International Airport, because I'm almost sure that my wallet was still there prior to customs—Someone picked my pocket! I discovered it when I tried to change some money to Euros. Looking confused the young woman behind the glass asked, "Are you okay sir?"

"My wallet's been stolen!"

"Unfortunately, it happens all the time here, and the police seem to do very little to stop it."

"Oh, that's great. It's a good thing I always have two wallets, both with money and credit cards when I travel, and keep my passport in a safe place, so I'm not destitute." Searching through my carry-on bag I found my second wallet, removing some cash to use for the exchange. While handing the money through the small opening at the bottom of the glass window I asked, "You seem to have encountered this problem before, so who should I report it to?"

"Even though I mentioned that the police do not seem to do anything to stop it, they've gotten better since the terrorist risk. A few years back I think they were the thieves or working with them, but now it's worth reporting, and be sure to call now to cancel your stolen credit card. What type is it?"

"VISA."

Searching a list on her desk she wrote down the number. "You can see that I've encountered your problem before."

"Clearly."

"You're clever dividing your money and credit cards, but unless you did that twice, you've only got one set left, and still have to report the theft to the police and make it out of the airport. Consider it an Olympic event with the hurdles being thieves. Also, don't assume that if police are with you it won't happen, as the thieves might only see that as an opportunity given how you're distracted."

"Nice welcome to your country, that is except for you."

With a warm smile and a wink, she replied, "Welcome to Greece."

Moving to a corner near the money exchange, where I could survey anyone approaching, I repacked my second, and last wallet, as deep in my carry-on bag as possible, and secured the bag over my shoulder. Only an "Act of God" could remove it now. Completing this defensive step, I called the credit card company and reported the theft, ensuring that my card is cancelled. I then reported the theft to the airport police who seemed completely disinterested. Since I had not yet decided on a hotel, I just gave them my phone number. I suspect that I have as much chance hearing from them as becoming a Greek God. It's a good thing that most of my cash is in my backup wallet.

Picturing everyone to be a thief, I worked my way over to the hotel advertisement area, and quickly called a couple of the more promising prospects. Fortunately, the second one I called, located near the historic sites, offers a good rate and for a higher floor; I do not want a lower floor with the increased risk of theft. Once in the cab I felt safe, at least until the driver demonstrated his driving skill, but we did make it unscathed to what seems to be a very nice, although modest, hotel. To my enormous relief, the room has a very secure miniature safe.

Given how depressed the Greek economy is I had little trouble arranging a private tour for a reasonable rate. The man at the tour desk claimed that Aminta, a guide well known to him, is excellent. Since she is scheduled to show up at 9:00, I have ample time for a relaxing breakfast and stop back at the room. With the tour already paid for, I'm restricting my money to some Euros for a tip and extras. The remaining credit card is definitely staying in my room locked down.

Seeing Aminta I wish that I'm a Greek God, as she appears to be a Greek Goddess, with an olive complexion glowing from a face designed to radiate beauty. Her black hair perfectly framing and complementing her features. Not to be outdone by her face, her body also demonstrates perfection of the Gods and Goddesses, with clearly ample, although discretely hidden, breasts, and long inviting slender legs emerging from a skirt cut just above her knees. It appears that this day is going to make up for the shaky start.

Aminta seems pleased by my looks as well, holding my hand for that second or two longer than if she was less impressed. "I will be your guide today, and you have me all to yourself."

I wish that means beyond the tour, but I'm trying not to get my hopes up too high. "You certainly have my attention, and let's hope it's a long day."

"Long as in interesting. I do not wish for guests to wish the day to end."

"I'm certain it'll be interesting." I neglected to add that with her appearance a tour of a sewing factory would be interesting.

"With my private tours, I give people an option of what to see. Maybe you can let me know what you wish to see or learn."

"I'm interested in religion, and learning about the ancient Greek multiple God system. In the process, I want to visit the main sites, and in particular those that give information about their religious life."

"That's helpful to know, because most people only want to see the ancient sites and learn a bit about them. Your focus is somewhat different. What I think is best is to visit the Acropolis and discuss religion as we tour the site."

"Lead the way."

Lead the way she did to a very nice street with cafes and restaurants at the base of the Acropolis. This will be an ideal place for a late lunch after the tour.

"Ready for a bit of a hike?"

"Yes, water bottle in hand and looking forward to it." I followed her up the hill, before long passing into an area with trees, providing welcome shade. Emerging from them we veered to the right and soon were at the top. The view is one not to be missed, with the ancient site on one side and the city of Athens sprawled out on the other.

"I wanted you to see this before explaining that the term "acropolis" translates into "high city," as now you can see why."

"That's for sure."

"We are about 500 feet, or 150 meters above Athens. This 7 or so acre site was a natural place to build on, as it is easy to defend. There is archeological evidence of settlements going back to almost

2,000 BC, with more complex structures later on. Prior to visiting most people think only of the Parthenon, as there are so many pictures of it out there, but this famous structure is only the center piece. Under the guidance of the general and statesman Pericles, construction began in 447 BC, employing the best craftsmen of the period and many unskilled laborers. Phidias who was the greatest sculptor of their time was hired, and he is said to have largely directed the show."

"Your mention of "show" is appropriate because from what I can see the whole site shows very well to the city of Athens."

"It does because it was built to fit around and on the hill as a natural extension. Do you know who it was built for?"

"Pericles?"

"The answer ties into your religious focus, as it was built for Athena, the Goddess presiding over Athens. The Parthenon was known as the "Temple of Athena Parthenos," or "Athena the Virgin," and she also has other smaller temples on the Acropolis. The ancient Greeks had many Gods and Goddesses, with Athena being a major one."

Approaching the Parthenon, I realize that it really is a shrine. Despite deterioration and large blocks strewn about, there is a special quality. "In my travels, I've seen several famous sites, but there's something unique about this one that I can't quite identify."

"It's the symmetry and perfection of the building style, with the Parthenon the best example. There are two rows of eight columns on either end and seventeen columns on the sides, all perfectly aligned. The interior has smaller columns, also perfectly aligned and styled. The structure has been heavily damaged over time, and is undergoing another round of restoration."

"Yes, I can see how the symmetry does make it so striking even in its less than ideal shape. I suppose the Goddess Athena couldn't protect it."

"Well, who's to say as the Parthenon has survived for so long. Imagine modern day buildings over such a period of time."

"Good point."

"Let's see the lady." Noting my puzzled look, she quickly added, "An amazing statue of Athena is inside what was the largest room." Moving to the interior that for the most part is open to the sky, we entered a massive restored room featuring a giant statue of the Goddess. The height, gold color, and lifelike facial expression impress, as I suppose was the intent.

"Striking isn't it, or perhaps I should say, isn't she?"

"Amazing!"

"This is a copy of the original as it was destroyed way back in antiquity. The one we're looking at was reconstructed from descriptions." Pointing to parts of the statue she added, "Athena is holding a statue of Victory in her right hand, the winged image. The shield and spear on her left side symbolize her role as protector of Athens."

"She must have been special to the ancient Greeks."

"Greek religion has several main deities, known as the twelve Olympians, with a king, Zeus, who resides on Mount Olympus. Scholars, though, do not agree fully on which of their Gods and Goddesses comprise this elite group. Each of the deities has special roles, such as Athena, the Goddess of war and wisdom, an interesting combination. She also rules over intelligence, skill, peace, and handicrafts."

"That's quite the mandate." I thought of the Egyptian Gods I encountered, and could see the multiple function role repeating. "It seems that females did well in ancient Greece as religious figures."

"Yes, that is certainly the case." A hint of pride came across in her words. "In addition to Athena there is Demeter, Artemis, Hera, Hestia, and of course Aphrodite. Demeter is the Goddess of food related matters, including agriculture, grain, harvest, growth, and nourishment. These roles give her power over the passage of a person through life and into the afterlife. Artemis is the Goddess of the hunt, wilderness, animals, young girls, childbirth, and plague. Hera is the Goddess of women, marriage, childbirth, kings, and empires, and also the Queen of the Gods. Hestia is the Goddess of the home, hearth, and chastity, and as such is a virgin Goddess. Aphrodite is the Goddess of beauty, love, desire, and pleasure, depicted as a very beautiful woman, and one having many lovers."

"Men must play into their system too."

"Of course, don't feel left out." Laughing she went on, "Men also have prominent roles as Gods in the ancient Greek system, with Apollo, Ares, Dionysus, Hades, Hephaestus, Hermes, Poseidon, and of course Zeus. Apollo is God of music, arts, knowledge, healing, prophecy, poetry, and plague. Ares is more negative being the God of war, bloodshed, and violence."

"I can only imagine the resume to qualify for that position."

"That's funny. Think of the qualifications for the next God, Dionysus, the God of wine, parties, festivals, drunkenness, chaos, madness, and ecstasy."

"I can think of many teenagers, and also adults for that matter, that qualify."

"Yes, so can I. Then there is the dark God, Hades, who rules the underworld and dead. Doesn't sound as much fun as Dionysus's role, does it?"

"No, but I guess quite an important role, given how religion always seems to have something to say about the afterlife."

"It's interesting that their central belief system mostly depicted the afterlife as an awful place ruled by Hades. Not the vacation destination of some religions, which is largely why cults arose to provide for a more pleasant afterlife, along with procedures required to get there. Before describing cult religion I'll finish telling you about the other main Greek Gods. I know it's a lot of information, but colorful."

"I find this fascinating, so please continue."

"Hephaestus is the God of fire, metalworking, and crafts, somewhat less interesting than Hades and Dionysus, but very important to their society. Also, very crucial to their way of life, Hermes is the God of travel, boundaries, communication, trade, language, and writing. Poseidon you've heard of I'm sure as the God of the sea, rivers, floods, droughts, and earthquakes. Then of course there is Zeus, the King of the Gods, ruler of Mount Olympus, and God of the sky, weather, thunder, lightning, law, order, and justice."

"Pretty much every aspect of their society and nature is covered by a major God."

"And there were quite a number of more minor deities that grew out of the cult religions, covering very specific things, such as Eros for love and attraction."

"So that's where the name comes from."

"When you hear the term "cult" you're probably thinking of some weird belief system, but for the ancient Greeks cult religions were the norm."

Smiling I commented, "That's kind of weird."

Missing my humor, Aminta continued, "From these cult religions they devised deities for every aspect of life, and also the afterlife. Then there are the stories involving the Gods, that give meaning to all aspects of their life. For example, the daughter of Demeter and Hades, Persephone, spends time with both her parents, much like modern day divorces I guess, and her return from the underworld to spend time with Demeter symbolizes the return of spring."

The simplified stories or parables of Christianity came to mind, Jesus perhaps taking a lesson from the ancient Greeks. "Simple stories accounting for various aspects of life and worship occur in other religions."

"They do, indeed. This was an age when there was no Internet, television, radio, and most people could not read. Entertainment often came in the form of stories about the Gods that could be easily recounted and acted out in theatres. Communities had their own unique plays depicting stories about their particular cult religion. There were actually thousands of these cult religions, with distinct Gods and Goddesses."

"Polytheism to the extreme."

"It was a way of distinguishing one community or area from another, and certainly allowed for a great deal of creativity. A key motivation though was to provide hope for a good afterlife, and not the one Hades had in store for them."

"There were different versions of the afterlife, then?"

"Yes, and the way into the cult religion and hence afterlife was often a mystery or secret, leading to the name "mystery" cults. For example, on the island of Samothrace initiates underwent an elaborate ceremony at night, that involved going from one special building to the next, starting with a gatehouse. From the gatehouse, they crossed a deep ravine symbolically separating the physical world from the spiritual one. Their next stop was a hall where sacrifices were made to the Gods. Sacrifices were considered to be a way of gaining assistance and avoiding punishment from the Gods. A frieze of dancing women suggests that this was also part of the ceremony. Finally, the initiates made their way to a large building where they were inducted into the religious cult. A theatre is located right beside this building highlighting how cult beliefs were acted out in plays. Unfortunately, we don't know much about their exact beliefs, given that it was a mystery cult, and it wouldn't have been much of a mystery if the answers were known to all."

"That initiation procession must have been quite a powerful experience to the initiates."

"You can just imagine how much so."

Realizing that we had been standing in the same place in the Parthenon for quite a while, I felt it was time to move on. "What else is there to see here?"

"There's the Erechtheion, one of the smaller temple to Athena I mentioned earlier." As we walked from the Parthenon to it she explained, "This temple actually sits on more sacred land than does the Parthenon. According to the story, there we go again with the story concept, Athena and Poseidon battled over who was to be the patron of Athens. Despite Poseidon making a spring burst forth by jabbing his trident into the ground, Athena was judged the victor by touching the ground with her spear and making an olive tree grow. You know us Greeks and our olives. The Erechtheion was built to honor her victory."

We stood facing a side wall still intact, with a small extension at the end. The columns on this smaller structure, connecting a lower wall to the roof, are also statues of Athena facing outwards. "Hard to miss who that's dedicated to."

"It was a busy place with festivals, sacrifices, religious processions, and games, in honor of Athena."

"Wouldn't it be amazing to be a fly on the wall and see what that was like?"

"I've fantasized about that myself, many times. They led a difficult life, but there were no shortage of festivals and celebrations, both major and cult."

"I hope they were not staged midday as it gets hot up here."

"That's why I like to do the tours in the morning or later in the day. Let's quickly see the remaining sites and then visit the museum, where you can see some of the pieces that have been discovered."

Following an hour or so at the surprisingly modern open concept museum, showcasing finds from the Acropolis and the area surrounding "the rock," we stopped for a late lunch on the street where we started our tour. I'm glad Aminta knows the restaurants as it would have been a difficult choice otherwise. It felt nice to sit down after the tour, and particularly so given the appeal of my guide.

"How have you found the tour? I always like to get feedback."

"Very good. I've had my fair share, or more than my fair share, of tour guides since I began to explore religions, and you're great at it. I like how you kept the focus on what I'm interested in, as I can see how you could orient the tour in many directions."

"I try as I've learned that guests appreciate hearing about topics that interest them. If I focus on pottery and they could care less, then I start to see their eyes cloud over as their mind drifts off. You seemed tuned in when we discussed the Gods and Goddesses."

"It's fascinating, particularly given the contrast to the monotheistic religions I've just explored—My Big 3 of Islam, Judaism, and Christianity. I can see pluses and minuses to both approaches."

"Such as?"

"Well, monotheism is definitely easier as you only have one God; I've not yet encountered one Goddess. On the other hand, it's kind of a one size fits all. The multiple God, or Goddess, system is harder to follow as there are so many players, but deities can be tailored to many purposes, some very specific, which has an appeal."

"Which do you prefer?"

"Good question. I don't know if I do, and I'm trying to remain neutral so I can learn in an objective way. If I say I prefer the single God system, then I might bias what I encounter about multiple God approaches."

"What do you think it all says about human nature?"

"There's so much information out there, even about single religions, that I can say we're a religious species. We appear to have a need to believe in something more than just this life. For your part, you've helped strengthen that notion by showing how when the main Greek Gods and Goddesses couldn't provide for a positive afterlife, cult religions formed to offer one. That's pretty strong support for religious beliefs providing us with hope for a good afterlife."

"I can see you're a thinker like me, always trying to analyze things."

"Yes, we do appear to have that in common. You also seem educated, and more than most guides. I'm a physician, an internal medicine specialist."

"I started my PhD in ancient history, but with our economic problems I couldn't get enough funding. Being a guide pays well, certainly compared to most jobs available in Greece now, and I get a chance to continue my education, although in a less formal way."

"I'm sorry to hear you had to stop your studies."

"Oh, I'll resume them."

"I can see you're determined like I am. We seem to have so much in common it would be a shame for me not to ask you out for dinner. How about it?"

Smiling she replied, "I always make it a rule never to date guests, but if I bent that rule it would be for you. Part of it too is my Greek Orthodox background with that nagging guilt thing. I guess it keeps me on track. What are your plans for the near future?"

"My next destination is Rome, not to learn about the Roman Catholic religion, but to learn about ancient Roman religion prior to Jesus."

"See, so you're moving on, and if I was to get attached, then I have to deal with the loss. It's one of the reasons I do not date guests."

"I see what you mean, and if I happened to get attached then the same would apply to me. Maybe we're getting ahead of ourselves because a dinner out doesn't necessarily mean a relationship."

"There's something about you, though, that makes me think it could. I'll tell you what, let's see a few of the more modern sites in Athens, and finish with an early dinner, and then when you move on we'll stay in contact. Who knows, if that works out then you can always visit for another tour." She added an inviting smile.

As anticipated the day continued to go well, ending with a nice dinner, and a growing sense of having a connection to Aminta, that she seemed to feel as well. I decided to take the high road, since as I like to say, the low road is so crowded, and not pressure her for more. Who knows, maybe I will be visiting Greece again.

ANCIENT ROMAN RELIGION

Compared to my arrival in Greece, Rome is a breeze, a possible omen? I don't consider myself to be particularly superstitious, though, so I'm not going to dwell on it. Any thoughts along this line passed quickly just by absorbing the energy of the city. As has been said, "When in Rome, do as the Romans do," so I got into the spirit heading to the Pantheon right after dropping my bags off at the hotel. This famous building is located in the city, almost just another structure except for the amazing design and history. From the front, it appears rectangular because the entrance, portico, and vestibule behind it have this shape. The triangular roof of the portico is supported by eight columns in the first row and two additional rows of four columns. I knew this even without walking right up to it from the travel guide I picked up. The guide book also informed me that the Pantheon was completed about year 126 after Christ, on the site of an earlier building, and that "Pantheon" translates into "temple of every God," clearly indicating the polytheistic nature of their religious beliefs.

During my explorations of religion to date, I went with the guided tour option, at least when viable, but not this time. I'm not sure why, but I think that Aminta and the magic of that day swayed me away from it. After all, how could another guide match up to her? Knowing my luck, it will be an old man who can barely speak English. Another reason is the turnaround time from the hotel to the Pantheon—There was no time to arrange a guide. I'm attributing the short time frame to the energy of Rome, but it could also be that I'm riding a wave of positive emotions from my Greek experience.

Entering the Pantheon, I passed through the rectangular vestibule into the rotunda, it having the distinction of being the largest unreinforced concrete dome ever. I read that the builders used increasingly lighter materials as they neared the top to lessen the weight bearing down on the foundation. A circular opening, apparently the largest ever created, lets in light and also rain, with the rain running off the slightly convex floor into ancient drainpipes below. I've seen some amazing buildings, and the Pantheon qualifies as one of the best, based on how the opening condenses sunlight into a beam that passes around the inside of the dome, as the Earth rotates each day. Totally ingenious as it brings the realm of the Gods right into the building! In addition, the height and diameter of the dome are exactly the same, giving those who stand in it a sense of ultimate symmetry. The order of Roman society embodied in this very unique structure.

At ground level, arches and recesses with statues convey a sense of activity in an otherwise empty structure. The activity is that of the Gods and Goddesses judging by the figures before me. However, without a guide I'm unlikely to learn much about their religion. Noting a very elderly man in a uniform I approached him, "Excuse me sir, do you speak English?"

"Yes, young man. What can I help you with?" His English surprisingly good but with a heavy accent.

"I'm interested in ancient Roman religion. Do you know much about it?"

"As an attendant, my job is to make sure people do not damage things, and watch for any trouble, but I've learned quite a bit over the years, so I can act as a guide for a small contribution."

Previously, I thought if I arranged for a guide I would end up with an old man, and I'm ending up with one after all. No uniformed personnel were visible that looked even remotely like Aminta. So it has to be. "What do you consider a "small contribution," and in what currency?"

"Euros will do, and the amount is what you feel in your heart."

"Okay, give me your best."

"Always, sir. Are you familiar with ancient Greek religion?"

"Fortunately, I was just in Greece and learned quite a bit about it."

"Good, because ancient Roman religion is more or less the same with the names changed."

Chuckling even though my guide was not smiling I ventured, "You've got to be kidding?"

"No sir. I can give you another story that many guides here do, but that is mostly how it is. The ancient Romans were very, how do you say, influenced, by the Greeks and their system of Gods and Goddesses. Like the Greeks they had their major Gods and Goddesses, and also numerous lesser ones that fulfilled all purposes."

"Well I guess that makes sense considering that the Romans came just after the Greeks, at least in terms of when their society was most powerful, and were next door neighbors."

"Also, the Greeks did so well with their Gods and Goddesses it would have been a waste to totally remake the system."

"What are some of the similarities and differences?"

"It is mostly in the names that there are differences, as the function is largely the same. The most powerful God for Romans was Jupiter, a change of name from Zeus. Other name changes occurred such as Dionysus to Bacchus, Demeter to Ceres, Artemis to Diana, Ares to Mars, Hermes to Mercury, Athena to Minerva, Poseidon to Neptune, Hades to Pluto, and Aphrodite to Venus. Apollo remained Apollo."

"They seem to have been big on planet names."

"More that we named our planets after their Gods."

"Of course, because many weren't discovered then. Astronomy wasn't my strongest subject."

"Yes." Honesty and directness evidently being one of my guide's qualities. "They had a Pantheon of twelve Gods and Goddess, like the Greek Olympians: Jupiter, Juno, Minerva, Vesta, Ceres, Diana, Venus, Mars, Mercury, Neptune, Volcanus, and Apollo. Memory is still pretty good, you see."

"Yes, I probably couldn't have listed all those."

"The Romans of the time also had many lesser deities, some overlapping with those of the Greeks."

"Are there are real differences between the Romans and Greeks?"

"Maybe in how religion was so connected to politics in ancient Rome, with no real separation. Political figures also were religious leaders, and all political acts of importance were appealed to the Gods, with a promise of devotion if the Gods ensured success. Like the Greeks, religion was part of daily life for everyone, and different regions often had their own Gods and Goddesses. They believed that aid from the Gods was required to achieve anything."

"What did they believe about the afterlife?"

"They believed that the soul is immortal, and upon death one is met by Mercury, the messenger God, who is also the son of Jupiter. Mercury takes a person's soul to the river Styx that flows nine times around the underworld. The person pays a fee to Charon, the ferryman, to take them across the river. This fee is not so much about money but about connection to the Gods or commitment. Across the river, they are judged to determine where they go. If a person was a warrior they go to the Fields of Elysium, and if not a warrior but good, go to the Plain of Asphodel. If the person committed crimes against society they go to Tartarus, where they are tortured by the Furies until their debt is paid."

"An eye for an eye sort of." The notion of Egyptian reciprocal treatment came to mind.

"Yes, and when the debt is paid in full they can proceed to a better afterlife. Pluto, brother of Jupiter, rules over all three regions. So even if they led a bad life they can still make it to a good place. Loved ones buried the person with a coin for Charon, and sometimes others things that might be needed."

"That's more positive than with the ancient Greeks."

"From what I've heard and read you're very right, as the ancient Greek afterlife was not so good, other than what the cult religions told them."

I thought of asking him what the various statues around the dome represent, but somehow don't feel like listening to all the stories I'll likely forget, and I'm concerned that my solid concise sense of ancient Roman religion will become confused. Beyond these reasons, I feel an odd urgency to leave the building, maybe because I'm still a bit too energized. I decided to wrap things up.

"I have to say that your knowledge is very impressive—I've learned a lot in a short time—and I like how you demonstrated that the Romans really built on the system created by the Greeks, while furthering it in some ways, like with the afterlife being more central and hopeful."

"I'm glad you enjoyed it. Some people see an old man and probably think, "Ah, what does he know, just an attendant," but I've heard and read a great deal through the years, and see the stories many guides give for what they are."

Handing him a generous payment, the generosity confirmed by his broad smile and strong handshake, I left the Pantheon wondering what my next step will be.

Walking across the crowded square fronting the portico, I recalled the Athens airport and the pickpocketing of my wallet. If modern day Romans follow in the footsteps of modern day Athenians, if that's even a proper word, then I'll have to be alert. This realization pushed thoughts about my next steps to the side or basement, and I began scanning everyone nearby. Close to the midway point, with the greatest concentration of people, I noted a young Middle Eastern male approaching, or appearing to approach me, his dress out of place given the long coat despite the heat. People do vary in their hot and cold tolerance though. I'd probably die in what he's wearing. When no more than a few feet away, he suddenly opened his jacket revealing explosives in a vest.

Reaching for a cord he shouted, "Death to the infidels," followed by "Allahu Akbar," with a crazed and/or stoned look in his eyes.

Realizing that this is the end I started to freeze, but thawed when nothing happened upon his pulling the cord. I can't say why I reacted as I did, since there did not seem to be any conscious thought process, but I rapidly took a step forward before the terrorist pulled the cord again, delivering a crushing punch to his nose. He probably would have reached for his nose given the amount of blood that shot out, except that he fell back cracking his head on the stone square and passing out, explosives still remaining unexploded.

My entire world had condensed to him, and so only gradually did I realize that others were about, most frozen in shock not having time to react given the speed of events. Some had thrown themselves to the ground while others started to move away, but most stood transfixed looking at me and my fallen adversary. Then I noticed a couple of police officers running in my direction with guns extended. They clearly had not seen what transpired, because they pointed their weapons at me. However, seeing the terrorist lying unconscious they holstered their guns and patted me on the back. One commented first in Italian, then in English when he noted my lack of comprehension, "Thank God for this."

They then directed everyone, other than myself, to leave the square. Even though I do not understand Italian, the movement of people following their instructions left little doubt about the meaning. When some remained standing the police officer who spoke to me commanded the remaining bystanders to leave, in English and then French. A middle-aged man approached flashing a badge, explaining first in Italian, then in English, that he is a detective who witnessed the whole event, recapping it for the officers.

One of the police officers stayed by the unconscious terrorist, the other officer and the detective escorting me back to the Pantheon. I felt safe by such a solid structure, knowing it had survived for almost 2,000 years. However, a strange sense of unreality and detachment accompanied the feeling of safety, that I recalled experiencing with the bus accident, "the horror," now seemingly so long ago. It's odd how feelings can transport you back in time.

Sirens helped connect me to the reality of the situation. Standing in the portico we watched as police cars, ambulances, and a bomb disposal truck arrived. While being questioned about exactly what transpired, I watched as a person, in what appears to be a space suit, approached the terrorist. After surveying the explosives for several minutes, he or she bent down and began working on them. In very little time at all the explosive belt was dumped in a very solid looking container that a colleague wheeled over. Once this container was taken back to the bomb disposal truck, the ambulance attendants and police descended on the terrorist.

Over the next couple of hours, additional police officers and someone from the anti-terrorism squad questioned me further. No one offered more than a bottle of water as I recounted yet again the very brief experience. Then came the reporters that I could see amassing at the edge of the square by the police barrier. I suppose the police have their favorites, as some were let through along with the photographers and camera people accompanying them. Once their questions were completed, the police sent me to the less favored media wolves. With such a short story and having recounted it so many times, I felt on auto pilot as I described what happened. My media experience after "the horror" must have helped because the questioning didn't disturb me at all, however the detached feeling likely also played a role.

Over the next several days the media storm continued, culminating in television appearances—A star first in North America and now in Europe! As with the former appearances I tried to keep it light adding humor, such as recounting how I thought I would die if I wore something as hot looking as the coat of the young terrorist. This piece played out well. I had to add humor as there was so little to the story from my perspective.

One of the positive aspects of these media spots was finding out information, as the police were very tight-lipped when I spoke to them again. I discovered that the man was from a local terrorist cell and that other members were just arrested. Apparently, they claimed that death to me would follow; I suppose blaming me for their incompetence in designing the belt was the easiest way, and they wanted death for everyone not of like beliefs. Hence, I do not feel special. Besides, the next 100 years they spend in jail will probably protect me.

Before long the inevitable came when a very composed middle-age female interviewer mentioned, "We've discovered that you escaped nearly certain death in a bus accident a while back. Also, from what we've learned the Policia cannot say why the explosives did not go off, as the belt appears to have been working."

This was news to me. "What are you suggesting?"

"Maybe you have some protective barrier around you."

"Or maybe I'm just lucky, and also young enough to react quickly and effectively, like by punching the terrorist."

"Ah, maybe, but are you sure?"

"I'm not sure that I can be sure of anything anymore."

Smiling my very direct interviewer continued, "Why are you in Italy?"

"Just visiting."

"According to a Policia source you are on a religious odyssey."

I guess the police do have their favorites, and I can image her getting information from a stone. I decided to be open, "After my first brush with death I began to wonder about the bigger picture, and have been travelling to learn about various religions. I started with ancient Egyptian religion, then Islam, Judaism, Christianity, ancient Greek religion, and now ancient Roman religion."

"What have you learned so far?"

"I'm still exploring so I can't say anything definitive, but I've certainly learned how there are both multiple God and single God systems, each very important to their followers. I've also discovered that people have a need to believe in a positive afterlife, much as I'm sure the man with the explosives does. However, he won't be encountering his heaven anytime soon, unless he considers three meals a day in jail to be heaven."

"With that explanation you are now teaching, so not just a student."

Yes, I realize that I fell head first into her trap.

"Perhaps you are a prophet!" She let the latter word hang to maximize the impact.

"You're really good at this, maybe too good, as I think you're creating your own storyline here. I do not see myself as a prophet, nor have I received any divine revelation while sitting on a mountain top, or for that matter the toilet in my hotel room. I'm just trying to sort it all out."

"Yes, and that is what prophets through the ages have done, and like them you will convey the message you've acquired."

Her words stunned me, as it was unlikely that I would discover some answer and remain silent about it. Fantasies of a book contract had crossed my mind, or at least a blog. Maybe expressing what I learned in one of these formats would make me a modern-day prophet.

Following this interview, I actually started receiving offers to write articles, and was contacted by a few book publishers. I informed all concerned that while very pleased at the prospect, I want to complete my exploration first, and then consider their offers so as to not bias my results. I realize that it is going to be difficult to move ahead with media attention, but feel reassured that their interest will fade given how media moves on to other topics very quickly.

Partly with the European media in mind, I decided to head back to North America right away. Another reason is that my funds are running low and it is time to earn more money. Even though there are other European-based religions, I learned from my readings that many of the other polytheistic (Pagan) belief systems of the region, such as Celtic and Norse, were highly influenced by Roman and later Christian belief systems. I want to concentrate on those that are more distinct, although Roman beliefs were largely taken from the Greeks as I discovered; quite a surprise. In addition, at least the Celtic religion was not well documented, as they did not write anything down, and accounts came later after it merged with Christianity.

As intended, I remained in contact with Aminta, indeed a few times a day while the media storm continued. She could barely believe what transpired, and said she wonders if there is truly some protective barrier, given the low probability of survival with both near death scenarios. Taking a humorous angle, I informed her that since I haven't been praying to any Greek or Roman God or Goddess, protection seems unlikely, but she still wasn't convinced. I certainly want to avoid a third near death experience as I move back to North America, and then onwards from there. My two nearly fatal experiences have led me to appreciate the value of life more than prior to them, and take each day for what it offers. Future days will hopefully offer additional insights into religion, and increasing closeness with Aminta.

MAYA RELIGION

After the media storm in Europe and its inevitable part two back in Canada, the storm in the Yucatan rainforest seems downright refreshing. Okay, so I might be a hero after the terrorist event, and maybe even the bus crash that now seems so long ago, but a "chosen" person or prophet? Maybe as a brief narcissistic fantasy to relieve the everyday realities of life, such as getting my wallet stolen in Greece, but to have a special religious role ongoing; I seriously doubt it. If I did, then why was my wallet stolen? Maybe it was all bad luck and timing, combined with very fast reflexes and the strength of my relatively youthful age. For sure, I wouldn't have survived either event as an old man. No one other than those aware of the two "miraculous" events, reacts to me as if I am special, and I certainly don't qualify as special in terms of getting patients to give up bad life style habits. Indeed, based on that criteria I might be deemed much less than special. The epidemic of obesity and diabetes plaguing much of the world, occurs despite our best efforts as physicians to try and convey the value of physical activity and weight control. Even suggesting that my special role might be to get that patient who smoked far too much to give it up, didn't work!

While back in Canada, largely to avoid the media, I decided to explore a few religions of the Americas that have prominent sites associated with them. The three that came to mind being the Maya of Mexico and central America, the Inca of South America, and the Anishinaabe of North America. Initially, I considered a Southeast Asia and Pacific Odyssey as my next step, but to afford it plus my ongoing expenses, I would have to work another few months. Besides, I really want to see some of the major sites of these three peoples. To experience Mayan religion authentically I booked myself into a nice lodge near to Chichen Itza, offering guided tours to this famous site.

Refreshed by the sound of the storm and fresh air that it brought, I awoke ready to go. Last night I met the four others in my small group set up by the lodge, a couple from Houston, and two men from Germany who appear to be in their forties. Travelling alone never bothered me, but it is nice to have companionship with like-minded people. Our guide, Eduardo, is from what we were told, one of the more experienced guides in the area, having run these tours for about thirty of his fifty or so years.

Entering Chichen Itza, Eduardo prefaced the experience in a way that I like, and find accurate based on my religious explorations to date, "The Mayan were, and actually still are, polytheists, meaning that they believe in multiple Gods. This is crucial to appreciate as we explore the site, because so much of it pertains to their religion."

"Here's the courtyard of Chichen Itza." We stood at the edge of a large grass clearing, my attention drawn to a pyramid at one end. I note that it vaguely resembles the Pyramids of Giza, but far more intact. Stairs on each side ascend to a temple at the top, different than the Egyptian ones that rise to a point, but both types seem to connect to the sky when viewed from the bottom.

Eduardo interrupted my reflections, "The pyramid we're facing is El Castillo, or "the castle." It is also known as the Temple of Kukulcan, the Feathered, or Plumed, Serpent God of War. At the base of the stairs are statues of Kukulcan's head. One of the most fascinating aspects of Chichen Itza is how on the spring and fall equinoxes, shadows in the form of a serpent's body appear beside the stairs on the northwest side, and connect to Kukulcan's head at the bottom. Some question whether this was a design feature or fluke, but it does occur only at the spring and autumn equinoxes, so I believe it was planned. The ancient Mayans were very good at astronomy, and the temples at the top of their pyramids often served as observatories."

The woman from Houston, Jean, commented, "I read that their Gods were very connected to the stars and planets, so I can see how this serpent shadow was part of the design."

"What's an equinox?" The question came from her husband, Ted.

"It's when the plane of the Earth's equator passes through the center of the sun, so that day and night are equal."

"Thanks, I never knew what that meant."

"For the Mayan people, science and religion were very connected, and their Gods were those of nature for the most part. In addition, their creation story has a very nature theme to it: The Earth is said to be created by Huracan, the God of the wind and sky. With only the sky and Earth there was no room for animals, people, or vegetation, an interesting way of looking at it. To rectify this problem, Huracan planted a Ceiba tree, with the roots through all levels of the underworld, and the branches into the upper world. The trunk grew to provide space for animals and plants. Initially, there were no people, and since the animals couldn't honor Gods, people were created."

Thinking of all the creativity I'd encountered in religions so far, I piped in, "That's quite the story, and as you mentioned, one very tied into the natural world."

"Yes, and it gets even more colorful, because they cited different epochs of people. In the first people were created of mud, but they were not able to think well, not surprising if you're made of mud. Realizing their mistake, the Gods destroyed the mud people with water, and produced the second epoch during which men were created from wood and women reeds. Unfortunately, these rather stiff people had no souls and again could not worship the Gods. If you're a God you find this unacceptable, and so they were destroyed by boiling hot water, with the survivors becoming monkeys. On the third go the Gods got it right and made people from maize. However, the first ones produced were too wise and a threat to the Gods, so Huracan clouded their minds and eyes so they would be less wise."

"How do they know this about the Mayan?" The question came from one of the German men, Fritz.

"The ancient Mayans were very sophisticated people, documenting many aspects of their life in hieroglyphics. This is so crucial because we then know who they were and what they did, and not just based on stories recounted by the Spanish conquerors."

"Can we climb the pyramid?" Fritz appeared eager to take on the challenge.

"Unfortunately, that has not been allowed for some time, as the number of people was adding greatly to erosion of the steps, and some were leaving graffiti. Both the many and few then ruined it for others. We can walk around it though. From having been to the top many times, I can say that it really is the view and not the pyramid itself, as nothing is in the temple at the top. Actually, one of the more interesting aspects of the pyramid, is how it was built over other temples, something the Maya people often did. In the 1930's an excavation from the top found another temple, with a statue of Chac Mool, and a throne in the shape of a jaguar painted red with inlaid jade. Chac was another prominent God, one of rain. We're going to see a statue of Chac Mool at the Temple of the Warriors."

Walking across the courtyard we arrived at the Temple of the Warriors. Passing between columns, we next climbed stairs to a platform where we encountered a reclining figure on his back, knees bent, head turned 90 degrees, and a flat stomach like a platform. "This is Chac. Does one of you wish to volunteer to be sacrificed?" Noting the looks of puzzlement and surprise he continued, "It is said that the flat section was where hearts of sacrificed humans were placed. A priest would make an incision below the ribcage, and with his hand tear out the heart of the sacrificed person while they were still alive."

An eerie and disgusted feeling settled over me with this information. I'd heard of these sacrifices by the Mayan people, but to stand right where still beating hearts were offered up feels weird. "How often did this occur?"

"No one knows for sure, but research suggests that it was not too common. More when times were really bad with very limited rainfall and more modest sacrifices, such as animals or corn, would not suffice. Often it was captured members of the ruling elite from an enemy society that were sacrificed."

"Maybe that's why it's called it the Temple of the Warriors." It seemed to fit with the sacrifice of captured enemies.

"Yes, that is one hypothesis. Sacrifices were also by beheadings and being thrown into cenotes, so not all were done by statues of Chac. Do you all know what cenotes are?"

Detecting uncertain looks Eduardo led us on a brief hike to a large circular depression with water at the base. "These natural fresh water wells were the lifeline of the Mayan people. Given how the ground is porous calcium carbonate derived from ancient reefs, there are no rivers or lakes. Rainwater passes underground, and these openings were and still are where the Mayan people acquire their water. At times children were sacrificed being thrown into the wells, the sides so steep that no one could emerge."

"Seems pretty cruel." I noted that sacrificial behavior was common in some of the religions I had encountered.

"True, but from their writings it appears that they believed that sacrifice was an honor, and a person who died in this way avoided the underworld where everyone else had to go. In addition, most pain was endured by the ruling elite, as bloodletting was the most common form of sacrifice. For women, this was often from the tongue and men from the penis. Strings were passed through incisions to maximize the bloodletting."

"Are you saying that women talked to much and men, well you know." I couldn't let the humorous aspect pass without a comment. Fortunately, it produced laughter amongst the group.

Smiling Eduardo commented, "I thought you were going to make reference to a sexual act involving the mouth and penis."

"Well that could be another interpretation."

When the laughter subsided Eduardo took us back to the main complex, to a court area with steep sided walls. Pointing to protrusions on the walls he explained, "Those extensions with holes were for a ballgame they played, on this the "great ball court," the largest of its kind, somewhat bigger than an American football field. Teams competed and points were made when a rubber ball passed through the hole." He led us to a carving showing a man being decapitated. "This demonstrates what happened to the losing team captain. Consider this outcome for a loss and professional teams now, with multi-million dollar contracts and only having to forfeit bonuses for losing performances."

"Life was rough in those days." It seemed to me that it was unnecessarily harsh.

"True, but think of the times in other areas. Mayan civilization arose around 250 years after Christ, and lasted as a dominant society until about 900 years after his death. Life was for the most part pretty good compared to many areas of Europe, or for that matter, much of the world. In addition, most of the people were farmers who probably had little to do with these temples, other than for special ceremonial days. For the average person, it was probably a good life, farming and watching the stars at night. Speaking of the stars, our last stop is the Caracol, their observatory."

At a small building, Eduardo led us up a curved passageway to the inner section of a dome containing three openings. "This is where the heavens were observed from. The Mayans loved their astronomy and were ahead of Europeans of the time. They made detailed observations of the sun, moon, Venus, and certain star clusters, linking them to their religion and daily life."

After the Caracol, Eduardo gave us time to walk around on our own. During my hike the thought arose that the Mayan, and certainly Egyptian, Greeks, and Romans, were motivated by their belief systems to produce amazing structures. The greatness of the structures aligning with the greatness of their Gods. Even with the monotheistic religions I've encountered, structures such as the Blue Mosque were erected to align with the greatness of a single God. One more insight and crucial piece of information added to my rapidly expanding knowledge of religion.

I spent another day in the region of Chichen Itza taking a rainforest hike, also with my small group, followed by two days of scuba diving at Cozumel off the coast of the Yucatan Peninsula, prior to moving on to another major Mayan site—Tikal in Guatemala—that is said to be characterized by even greater temple development.

Comparing Tikal to Chichen Itza, or for that matter, any other Mayan site, the one thing that stands out is the size of Tikal—It's immense! I read that it covers 575 square kilometers of jungle and temples. Many of the lesser temples and buildings still remain overgrown by rainforest. With Chichen Itza it is quite easy to get an overview of the site, and tour it in a short time frame, but not for Tikal, aside from flying over it. I anticipate seeing the main temples in my couple of days of exploration, but a person could spend much longer here and still find things of interest.

My guide, a pleasant and slightly overweight woman in her later thirties or early forties, met me by the entrance gate. Luciana stated that we will be seeing some of the temples this afternoon, and the remainder tomorrow morning. That suits me just fine.

Starting the tour right away she explained, "One thing that stands out about Tikal is the jungle, and how it almost competes with the temples for dominance. Tikal rose to prominence in the eighth century after Christ, and then like all other Mayan cities faded in the ninth century."

"Why did that happen."

"No one knows for sure, possibilities including drought, war, over-population. Personally, I believe it was excessive accumulation of wealth in the hands of the few, much like we're seeing these days. In modern day Guatemala, it's far worse than in first world nations. There's much corruption here, and leaders get rich along with the business elite, while many Guatemalan people suffer. I believe this is what also happened in the Mayan world, with the ruling elite and priest class taking much more than the average farmer or worker. After so long the whole thing likely imploded, as it might in our world. Maybe drought, war, or the other factors triggered it, but the root cause was the lack of balance."

"You seem to care a great deal about this." I was stating the obvious.

"Yes, I do and have studied it for my political science Masters. I think we all should be concerned, but so few seem to be."

"Actually, I share your sentiments, and feel it's all going somewhere we don't want to be going, even if you're a member of the elite. Remember history, with all those heads rolling in the French Revolution."

Realizing that I had similar sentiments, Luciana smiled broadly. "I like taking out guests who have a sense of social justice. Are you American?"

"No, I'm Canadian."

"Sometimes I've had rich Americans bragging about all their wealth, and I can't stand it."

"I can imagine it would be difficult for you."

"This will be an easier tour for me. Since I'm sure that you came to see the sites of Tikal, and not discuss politics, I'll be a good tour guide and provide some information about the ancient Mayan people who lived here."

"I'm looking forward to it."

As we walked into what I recognized from Chichen Itza as the courtyard, Luciana explained, "The two temples that you see as bookmarks at either end of the courtyard, known as the Great Plaza, are Temple 1 and Temple II. Temple I to our right has the narrow top. It's known as the Temple of the Grand Jaguar, housing the tomb of Ah Cacau, that can be translated as Lord Chocolate."

"Kids must have loved him."

"Unless he sacrificed them into a cenote. You know what a cenote is?"

"Yes, I just visited Chichen Itza."

"Good so you can compare the sites. Lord Chocolate was buried with pottery, sea shells and pearls for the afterlife."

"No chocolate?"

"Maybe, but he probably ate it waiting for his journey. The temple was built about 700 AD during his rule. From our position, you can see how steep the stairs are. Many people in modern times, and I'm certain in early times, have fallen. The Mayan constructed some temples such that the top was challenging to reach; an ordeal of sorts."

Looking at the steepness and also very small size of the stairs, I got the idea. "Ya, I can see how they could be lethal."

"Due to the accidents, park authorities have banned climbing it, but we'll go up Temple II, as the stairs are more reasonable, and you'll have a great view of Temple I. Both are about the same height, 47 meters for Temple I and 38 meters for Temple II. Tomorrow morning we'll ascend Temple IV at 65 meters, the tallest structure in the Mayan world."

The ascent of Temple II proved not that challenging, and Luciana is right—The view across the courtyard to Temple I is amazing. The small building at the top with the one entrance stands out more clearly, as does the prominence of the jungle. "The view is incredible, as you suggested."

"Wait until you see the view from Temple IV. The temple we're on is also known as Temple of the Masks, and was built by Lord Chocolate in honor of his wife." Laughing at her own humor in advance she added, "I guess he could have some distance from her in the afterlife."

Withholding any questions about the happiness of her romance, or romances, I commented, "That's an interesting way of looking at it."

"Maybe they just wanted to look at each other. That's one of the great things about history—You can interpret it in so many ways."

"Speaking of interpretations, why is this called the Temple of the Masks?"

"I should have pointed out the masks at the base of the stairway guarding the temple. We'll take a look when we descend." Shifting focus, she asked, "How many levels do you see in Temple I?"

Taking my time, I counted slowly before responding. "It appears there are nine."

"Yes exactly, the levels representing those of the underworld, although set above ground."

"Wouldn't it have been interesting if they constructed an inverted pyramid into the ground descending nine levels?"

"That's an amazing notion. I suspect that there would be a massive flooding problem with the underground water, and also who would stand in awe of a building that is underground. The rulers wanted their buildings to reach towards the sky and be admired by all."

"An underground temple would not be so easy to admire, for sure. What about the realms beyond the underworld?"

"The ancient Maya believed that there is one level to the middle world, and thirteen to the upper world. Have you encountered the creation story?" Seeing me nod Luciana continued, "The Ceiba tree grows through all the levels acting as a natural connection."

"I heard from my Chichen Itza guide that everyone goes to the underworld."

"Except those who are sacrificed or die in childbirth. The underworld is said to be populated by evil Gods. However, another belief arose that those who follow the Goddess Ixtab go to a paradise."

"This seems to be a common theme: When a religion like that of the Greeks or Mayan people does not provide for a positive afterlife, more hopeful options are generated, such as with the cult religions of the ancient Greeks."

"That's interesting, and it makes sense. People want to believe in something positive, particularly if their life is stressful."

"The only deities I've heard about are Kukulcan, Huracan, Chac, and now Ixtab. What about the others?"

"There is the maize God, Hun H'unahpu, who some Mayans believe created the world. The various Gods have roles, and also names, that varied depending on the particular region of the Mayan empire. They also have overlapping functions with other Gods and Goddesses. K'awil, or just God K, as the protector of the royal line and God of lightning, is one of their more important deities. Kisim is the God of death and decay, often described as the "flatulent one," not for what emerged from his behind, but for his role in death. On a brighter note, Ix Chel is the Goddess of rainbows, although the

Mayans often believed that they brought bad luck. The God of all creation is Itzam Na, but oddly little is known about him."

"So basically, the Gods and Goddesses served various functions tied into the Mayan way of life."

"Exactly, as with other multiple God systems."

Gazing at the view from Temple II, Luciana asked, "What else do you see from here?"

Focusing my attention, I noted various other smaller structures, some still overgrown. "There seems to be many other parts to the complex."

"There are two main parts—the ceremonial and residential sections—each with terraces and pillars known as stelae. It was a very active city."

"Odd how it just collapsed so fast."

"That's the way that nature and even human societies work; they endure and when stress becomes too great they fade fast."

"From what I've encountered I think you're right, although some things like these buildings do persist."

"They do, but the area was so overgrown with jungle that in the sixteenth century the Spanish passed right by and missed the site!"

"Shows how strong nature is."

On the way down I paid more attention to the construction, noting that it was built in layers with stairs on one side; very different than Temple I. I also took note of the masks I somehow missed on the way up, probably because I was focused on the stairs and the top.

The next morning consisted of a hike around the Tikal complex, but only a fraction of the total area according to Luciana. We observed tower-like Temple III, the Temple of the Jaguar Priest, standing taller than Temple I at 55 meters. Luciana explained that it holds the tomb of King Dark Sun.

The most amazing part of Tikal, and probably the whole Mayan experience, proved to be our climb up Temple IV; the exertion rewarded by a view of the rainforest seemingly stretching to infinity, only interrupted by the temple summits poking through. It triggered a fantasy of being a bird and soaring over the rainforest from one temple to the next. I made the climb to the roof of the temple room, braving the narrow ledge right around the perimeter, to take in the 360-degree panorama. No railings safe guarding against a fall to certain death. I know I'll never forget that image from the top, so potent that its etched into my psyche.

One of the most striking aspects of visiting both Chichen Itza and Tikal has been to see how extensive the Mayan empire was—It spanned an enormous region. Luciana mentioned that after its downfall many of the Mayan beliefs continued in various forms, and were influenced by Christianity brought by the Spaniards. Modern day Mayans still follow many of the ancient beliefs. This was another thing I learned: That beliefs do tend to persist and influence newer ones. I shared this with Luciana, and also Aminta later when we face-timed in the afternoon after the tour,

"I find it fascinating how past perspectives carry on, like with the ancient Mayan concepts influencing modern day Mayan people, and the Roman beliefs derived from those of your ancestors in Greece."

"What other common themes have emerged?"

"Well, there's the creativity involved in religious beliefs, and how the stories provide a meaning and purpose to life, and explain natural events, such as death. From this function, a connection to nature and hope for a good afterlife follow. Then there's how religions have prompted the creation of stunning building projects, that align with the power of their Gods and Goddesses, or just God with the monotheistic Big 3. On the more negative side, sacrifice of some form seems to be required, but it was often viewed in a positive way, highlighting how interpretations can vary."

"I think that you will have to stop learning or you will be guiding me at the rate you're going."

"That might be a shame because I appreciate your guiding so much."

"There is more to learn in Greece so maybe you have to make a second visit, reserving me from the start."

"Now that's great guidance, but first I have to complete the search for answers here and in the far east."

"I feel that you will succeed if you continue to learn so well, and I so much wish for this to happen."

Aminta's last words heightened my sense of curiosity and confidence, and I do realize how much I have advanced in my understanding. With a little luck and much perseverance something will emerge, I know it.

INCA RELIGION

Being a medical doctor I should have realized that the altitude of Cusco, Peru—almost 4,000 meters or just over 13,000 ft.—was going to trigger Acute Mountain Sickness. I even packed acetazolamide, a medication that speeds up breathing and counters the illness. Thinking, "I (the hero, as if) will be okay," I decided to postpone taking it, and what a mistake. Shortly after arriving I started to feel lightheaded, groggy, nauseated, weak, and downright horrible. I checked into a modest hotel booked at the airport, and it was just after getting to my room that I really started to feel sick. Unpacking the acetazolamide, I started my first dose. Unfortunately, the medication needs to be taken a few days before arriving for maximum benefit, and playing catchup with it is far less effective. Calling the hotel reception, I explained my state, the helpful clerk suggesting that room service send up some coca tea. Apparently, coca leaves as a tea counter altitude sickness. Eager for some immediate relief I started drinking the very down to Earth, if not soil like, tasting liquid. Hopeful that relief is on its way I laid back on the bed.

Two hours later my symptoms are not a bit better, but I'm now on the toilet in full diarrhea mode, likely from the tea. If only they put these experiences in the glossy travel magazines. I recall reading in the travel guide I purchased, that the Hotel Monasterio offers oxygen enriched rooms to counter altitude sickness. Aware that my current hotel does not have such rooms, I called the more luxurious hotel when my bowels took a break. Fortunately, an oxygen enriched room is available. Showing understanding and some empathy, the clerk at my first hotel only charged me a half-day rate, the tea on the house. To counter the diarrhea, I downed an Immodium tablet; never travel without them as I say. Medicated up, and hopeful my bowels will hold out, I took a brief cab ride to the Hotel Monasterio.

Lying on the luxury bed knowing that the enriched oxygen will shortly restore normal functioning, I feel a great sense of relief, even though I'm still feeling horrible. Four days from now I'm scheduled to arrive at the Sanctuary Lodge right at the ancient Inca site of Machu Picchu. This is a good thing because Machu Picchu is only 2,400 meters, or about 8,000 ft., above sea level, the altitude where Acute Mountain Sickness just starts. So, with the medication onboard, an oxygen enriched room, particularly important at night when the main impact of the illness occurs, and travel to a lower altitude shortly, I realize things will work out.

Many unprepared travelers arrive in Cusco, unaware of Acute Mountain Sickness, and start hiking the Machu Picchu trail, ascending even higher than Cusco at sections. Not surprisingly, many suffer and some have to be carried off the trail. With limited time, and also hearing from a friend how nice it is to stay right at the Machu Picchu site, I opted in advance to skip the hike and take the train. My purpose is learning about Inca religion, and a trail hike over a several days will not advance that aim.

Given my physical and mental state—Acute Mountain Sickness impacts on mood demonstrating the mind-body connection—I opted to relax for a couple of days at the hotel. In earlier times the hotel was an actual Spanish colonial working estate, with an authentic courtyard, and white cloisters where the restaurant is now nestled. Taking it easy with meals, I ate slowly enjoying the view of the courtyard, while reading. The hotel library has some good reads, particularly about the Inca. One chapter in a book about Inca beliefs is holding my attention, as it describes their creation mythology.

Inca religious beliefs were very influenced by both earlier and contemporary, to their time, Andean peoples. This is understandable given that the Incan empire really only lasted about 100 years. From about 1,200 to the early 1,400's AD, the Inca were just one of several civilizations battling for supremacy, and seemed to fair no better than their rivals. Then around 1438 AD the Inca ruler, Viracocha and his son, Pachakuti, defeated the Chankas. Following this success other local civilizations were conquered, and campaigns were launched into Bolivia, with Lake Titicaca being a key site. Under Pachakuti and his successor, Topa Inca, the frontier expanded an amazing 4,300 miles from Chile to the Ecuador-Columbia border, and incorporated modern day Peru, Bolivia, Ecuador, northern Chile, and northwestern Argentina. Then with the Spanish Conquistadors the Inca empire collapsed in 1532. This 100-year period would not be enough to establish a fully novel religion, and beliefs were drawn from the various civilizations, although the Inca religion developed into a unique brand.

According to the Inca belief system, the creator God, Viracocha began the world on the Sacred Island of the Sun on Lake Titicaca. Viracocha initially produced a race of giants, but realized that they were too large, and then made humans. These first humans, though, turned out to be greedy and arrogant, so Viracocha punished them by turning some to stone, and others into soil and vegetation. Hence, the natural world is formed from humans, literally! The creator God then unleashed a great flood to wipe the world clean, leaving only three people to start the race again. Considering the story, I reasoned that these three would be highly motivated to act decently given what happened to all the others.

Viracocha also created the sun, moon, and stars. Now that's one busy God. The creation story takes an interesting turn at this point, with Viracocha disguising himself as a beggar and travelling around, going under the name of Kon-Tiki. During his journeys, he made carvings at various locations and created Cusco by having the founding couple—Manco Capac and Mama Ocllo—settle there. If all this was not enough, Viracocha taught people civilized arts before walking into the sea, promising that one day his messengers would return. I suppose that the ruler, Viracocha, felt that he couldn't go wrong taking the name of their creator God, and in a sense created the Inca empire!

Finding the creation story so absorbing I continued reading on, almost oblivious to the passage of time. The Inca had many other Gods and also Goddesses, with one of the most prominent being the Sun God, Inti, who was also patron of the empire and of conquest. A High Priest (Villaq Umu) served Inti along with young virgin priests, the acllas. Inti had temples in each town, and even land reserved for him. A festival—Qhapaq Ucha—honored both Viracocha and Inti, with towns expected to send one or two good-looking children to be sacrificed in a ceremony in Cusco, or at other sites along a pilgrimage route. Strangulation or having the heart removed was the method of death. The sacrifices were believed to guarantee the well-being of the leader and the empire. Yes, incredibly cruel, and you can only imagine the fear in those children and loss for the parents, but it seems that all religions require some form of sacrifice whether it be animals, people, or Jesus dying for all others. The hierarchical structure to deities that I initially learned about in Egypt is an additional theme: If there are multiple Gods and Goddesses they have different rankings, from the supreme one, to the powerful deities, to the lesser ones. In a single God system, the deity is all powerful, and far more so than humans.

Reading on I discovered that Cusco was the heart of the Inca empire, and the most sacred site, Coricancha, is not far from my hotel. Coricancha has temples to Inti, Viracocha, and the other major Gods, including the moon Goddess Mama Kilya, Illapa the thunder God, Ciuchi the rainbow God with rainbows being seen as bad omens like with the Mayan people, and Chaska-Qoylor the Goddess of Venus. The Inca also had lesser deities, such as the earth Goddess, Pachamama, honored by farmers, and Mamacocha, Goddess of lakes and the sea, worshipped by coastal people. Demonstrating how Inca religion was derived from belief systems of civilizations drawn into their empire, Pachamama, was worshipped long before the Inca dominated.

Pachamama had a central role as the earth mother in the lower realms of ukhu pacha and urin pacha. Hanan pacha, the upper realm, includes deities of the sun, moon, stars, rainbows, and lightning. People occupy Kay pacha between the upper and lower realms, similar to the Mayan belief system. A key aspect of Inca religion is that of duality of the Cosmos, with the upper and lower realms. If a person leads a virtuous life, he or she joins the sun and participates in the lives of descendants. The living often brought food and gifts to mummified dead to maintain the connection. If a person leads a bad life, then he or she is condemned to a desolate and cold eternity in the underworld. Once again, the theme of good and bad afterlife options, depending upon how a person conducts themselves in this life.

Feeling overwhelmed by all the information about Inca Gods and Goddesses and their mythology, and also feeling better physically and mentally by the third morning, I decided to take a break from reading. Cusco itself has some interesting sites, such as Coricancha, right in the heart of the city. I note that my breathing rate has increased markedly, obviously from the acetazolamide. Headaches, nausea, and shortness of breath are more or less gone, and my bowels are fine. At the central plaza of Cusco, the Plaza De Armas, I marveled at the old-style colonial architecture, before stopping for a coffee in a second-floor restaurant. From my railing seat overlooking the courtyard, I see tourists blending with local business people, and even some individuals in traditional Peruvian dress, such as women wearing patterned woven shawls. Everyone appears so relaxed; perhaps the altitude makes excessive exertion difficult.

Ready for some sightseeing I walked the short distance to Coricancha. Looking at it from the road my impression is not great, due to the Santo Domingo monastery the Spanish built on top of the Inca site, to assert that the Roman Catholic religion had indeed replaced the Inca belief system. I recall this from my readings yesterday. The Inca site was built by the ninth ruler, Pachacuti Inca Yupanqui, on an earlier site. Entering the temple complex, and trying to ignore the Spanish replacement structure, it strikes me that I'm standing at the very heart of the Inca empire. From above, Coricancha resembled (prior to the monastery) a sun with rays shining out. The rays represented the forty-one sacred ceque, connections to numerous sacred sites throughout their empire. At one section branching lines in the floor curve back towards each other, symbolizing the duality of their cosmos.

Most striking is the stonework in the still mostly preserved inner temples. The Inca were masters at construction, fitting huge blocks together without mortar, such that even a thin pocketknife can't penetrate the joints. The smoothness of the stones and tightness of the joints is a wonder of architecture and construction. Inca builders even worked out how to prevent damage from earthquakes, by having the walls tilt slightly inwards with height, and doors and windows trapezoid narrowing from bottom to top.

Temples to their prominent Gods and Goddesses were constructed around a central courtyard at Coricancha. These temples are still intact, but gold and silver paneling and artifacts were taken by the Spanish and melted down for ingots. You can only imagine the sense of defeat and humiliation the Inca must have felt. In contrast, I thought of how the ancient Greeks and Romans incorporated religions of the regions they occupied, but then the systems were polytheistic. I suppose there is no real compromise between polytheistic and monotheistic.

At the Temple of the Sun, dedicated to the Sun God Inti (who else), I recalled from my readings at the Hotel Monasterio how a gold statue of Inti went missing, presumed to have been melted down by the Spanish, although no one knows for sure. From Inti's head and shoulders sun rays shone, and the stomach of the statue stored ashes from the vital organs of Inca rulers. The interior and exterior walls of Inti's temple were covered in sheets of gold, considered to be the sweat of the sun. If this was not enough worship in precious metal, the garden of the temple was made of gold and silver, including a field of corn, and life-size models of jaguars, llamas, shepherds, guinea pigs, monkeys, birds, and even butterflies and insects. All gone, melted down.

Visiting the other internal temples, I tried to visualize how impressive the courtyard surrounded by temples would have been without a monastery superimposed upon it. The temple to the moon Goddess was covered in silver, the contrast with the gold of Inti's temple, undoubtedly being very striking. Indicating how the Inca revered their dead, mummified remains of former Inca emperors and their wives were stored and brought out during special ceremonies.

Recalling how Coricancha is part of a larger design, a puma with the temple complex corresponding to the genitalia, and the head represented by a fort on a hill overlooking Cusco—Sacsayhauman—I decided that my next stop will be this site. The mostly uphill walk is invigorating, and it reminds me that I still have not acclimatized fully. Nasty dogs challenging me along the route are not helping with my breathing. Wishing I'd opted for a cab ride, I suddenly arrived at the fort.

What is most striking about this amazing military structure is the jagged walls, supporting terraces now covered in grass. I don't recall ever seeing a structure like it. Thinking that this might be the puma's head, an image not clear from the site, I imagined these could be teeth, but in three ascending rows? Although it appears to be a fort, there is some suggestion that it was not designed as such, more to convey the power and mastery of the Inca and/or as a temple to the sun God, Inti. No one knows for sure. As impressive as they are from a distance, the zigzagging walls are more formidable at ground level, dwarfing mere people looking up at them. If nothing else the Inca were certainly creative with their architecture and religious beliefs. From the top terrace, Cusco sits below me sheltered by the surrounding hills. A giant statue of Christ looks down on the town from one hilltop; at least it wasn't built on Sacsayhauman.

The two days of rest and reading, followed by a day of light touring and walking yesterday, put me in the mood for the train ride to one of the most famous sites in the world—Machu Picchu. Since I'll be returning to the Hotel Monasterio after a couple of nights at Machu Picchu, I left most of my luggage in the storeroom, and packed a smaller bag for the brief excursion. The train further got me into the mood, it resembling that from an old and largely forgotten era, and while lacking in modern amenities, the atmosphere more than compensates.

    The first part of the train journey starts out somewhat odd with zigzagging back and forth. I thought something was wrong with the train, until a passenger seated next to me explained that the train has to go through a series of switchbacks, as the elevation is too great for a direct route on the hills around Cusco. After this slightly unnerving train experience, we began rolling along the Urubamba Valley, or as it's often called, Sacred Valley, with lush fields, some on terraced slopes like in the days of the Inca. It takes little imagination to appreciate the value of this valley to the Inca, given how the steep hills bordering it would have presented challenges for growing crops, and rainfall makes the valley lush and fertile. The Urubamaba River coursing through the valley also satisfies water needs. Not a bad place to live, unless you were slated for sacrifice of course.

    Departing the train, I took my time observing the colorful locomotive and people to the sides of the tracks. Since my check in is for 4:00 PM at earliest and small travel bag light, I decided to walk around the town, and ended the tour with a late relaxing lunch. From the town, Machu Picchu is not visible at all, a good thing because the Spanish conquistadors totally missed it, never discovering its location. Machu Picchu is situated on a plateau between two mountain peaks, about 450 meters, or 1,500 feet above the Urubamba River. Eager to reach the famous site, I boarded a bus to the top just after 4:00 PM. My room, although not as luxurious as at the Hotel Monasterio, is very comfortable. Given that the sun will be setting soon, I opted to take a short stroll into the ruins staying near the entrance, really just wetting my appetite for tomorrow.

Wanting to get an early start, I got up quickly and finished breakfast prior to sunrise. Entering Machu Picchu an hour later hoping to see it basking in the rising sun, I'm only seeing fog covering the whole site. Noting my surprise, an attendant at the gate explained that this is common through much of the year, and a real disappointment to those finishing the trail. As the fog lifted with the steadily rising sun, I strolled deeper into the site. Having read so much that first day in Cusco, it seems best to make my own way through the ruins. With clear visibility, I easily distinguish the terraced agricultural section from the urban section, and also upper and lower towns. My first main stop is the Sacred Square above the Central Square, where the Intihuatana stone is located.

The first thing catching my attention is how this stone stands out from everything else: The vertical rectangular shaped rock with a sloping base is perched on an elevated platform, in turn on a flat surface within the Sacred Square. The distinct placement and design matches the unique function of "the hitching post of the sun," as the Inca believed that it holds the sun in place along its annual path. Given that Inti is the sun God, it makes sense that it be named for him. Midday on November 11 and January 30, the sun is right above the stone such that no shadow is cast. On June 21, the summer solstice, when the location on the horizon of the setting sun stops and then reverses, the shadow cast on the southern side of Intihuatana is the longest of the year. On December 21, the winter solstice, a much shorter shadow occurs on the northern side. Absolutely amazing what the Inca figured out and how they translated that knowledge into unique architecture, as I recall noting with other ancient civilizations.

My next stop, the Temple of the Sun, in the upper urban section, is another example of very unique architecture. The semi-circular walls mark it as a distinct building, and up close the special nature is evident from the absolute precision of the seams and perfect trapezoid windows. The "Torreon," or tower, was built on elevated granite to ensure that it stands above the surrounding buildings. Only members of the royal family and high priests were allowed access, commoners such as myself being kept out by a gate. Most ceremonies of significance were probably conducted at this location. Beneath the tower is an underground chamber, that likely contained the remains of rulers.

Leaving the urban section, I'm now entering the terraced agricultural section. With the lower elevation of Machu Picchu, acetazolamide on board, and time to acclimatize, the walk to the top is effortless. At the Watchman's Hut, the terraces stretch out below with their rock walls and flat areas that used to hold crops. The Inca architects and builders designed a unique water flow system, such that they could regulate where water went. At the same point in time people were tossing their crap out of windows in many European cities lacking sewage systems, unless as a carry-over of the ancient Romans. Meanwhile, the Spanish were persecuting the Inca, likely considering them to be inferior.

The Inca trail from Cusco ends at the top of the agricultural zone, and for that classic view of Machu Picchu I decided to walk up the trail. At a substantially higher elevation I ate the lunch prepared for me by the Sanctuary Lodge restaurant staff. I can't recall ever having such a view with lunch. Since almost everyone ends the hike in early morning, to encounter Machu Picchu in fog, something the trail guides eager to get back home often fail to explain from what the attendant told me, I had the trail to myself. In the midst of the site the structure is fairly clear, if you've read about it, but from above everything is laid out, including the sister peak to Machu Picchu, Huayna Picchu, behind the city that is clearly perched on a plateau.

Most striking is the merging of natural and man-made forms, the terraced fields of the agricultural section spilling down the slope, and the positioning of buildings and plazas on flatter sections, although both upper and lower towns descend, seemingly off the side. Developers might be less impressed given that sprawl wouldn't work out too well. From the information I've absorbed, the reason why Machu Picchu was constructed is not clear, some believing that it was an agricultural project, others a guard post against rival groups from the rainforest world at lower elevations, and still others a temple to Inti. Although different motivations might apply, gazing down at this most amazing of sites with the sun shining down on it, I believe the latter perspective wins. Inti would indeed be very impressed at what was constructed, and both the Temple of the Sun and Intihuatana support the theory that it was mostly a temple to him.

Pleased that I've actually visited Machu Picchu and put it into perspective, I returned to the main site and ambled around the urban section before returning to the Sanctuary Lodge. A nice middle-aged couple joined me for dinner, the chance to discuss what I've seen being greatly appreciated.

Next morning, I took another stab at viewing the site at sunrise, but once again fog. I quickly visited some of the places missed yesterday, before returning, packing, and checking out. My train back to Cusco is booked for late morning. An odd mixture of elation and sadness came with departing, something I attributed to seeing, and now leaving, what is arguably the most amazing blend of natural and man-made scenery in the world!

Fortunately, one more day of touring around Cusco remains, this time to the town and fort of Ollantaytambo, plus an excursion to an authentic small town at a higher elevation. I booked this bus tour at the Hotel Monasterio, and now boarding I feel anxious. I guess I'm still apprehensive about bus trips. On the way to the site the tour guide explained that Ollantaytambo enabled Manco Inca Yupanqui, leader of the Inca resistance to fend off an assault by the Spanish for a time. Arriving at Ollantaytambo and looking up the terraced slope, I can see how he succeeded. I'm not a military person, but defending from a higher elevation seems obvious. In addition, the resistance leader used the Inca water flow system to flood fields that the Spanish were fighting from forcing them to retreat.

Climbing the path beside the terraced slopes makes you appreciate just how high and steep the site is, and how impossible it would be to attack from below. The terraced fields remind me of Machu Picchu, briefly triggering that odd mix of elation and sadness again. With the town of Ollantaytambo below, "Temple Hill" is truly a fort and also temple. Unlike Machu Picchu, the site was not fully completed, and some very large stones lay discarded at the top by the Temple of the Sun. It appears that Inti more than claimed his fair share of temples.

The tour guide explained that the Temple of the Sun served as a calendar marking the summer and winter solstices. The structure that I and most others, judging from the reaction of those around me, find most striking, is the Unfinished Wall of Six Monoliths, containing six (of course) very tall rectangular stones, joined with perfect seams lacking mortar. So tight are the seams, that a pin cannot fit between these 50 ton blocks! Apparently, it was designed to be the prominent part of the Temple of the Sun. A very unique doorway with both a wider and narrower section, also adorns the temple.

Taking us to the side of the temple complex, the guide pointed to a gradually sloping road. She explained that this is how the pink granite, mined in the mountains we are looking at, was transported to the site. She also pointed at caves up the slopes that were for grain storage, the cool air keeping the grain dry and fresh, and also safe from animals. The agility required to transport grain back and forth to these caves on steep narrow trails is almost inconceivable, as is the work required to carve the deity, Wiracocha, into the cliff face. I can make out a pointed hat on his head, and heavy packs on his back. What the Inca established in such a short time can only be described as near impossible, and it highlights something I've observed in my travels to date: That societies can achieve remarkable, seemingly almost God-like things, when it all comes together, but this state of affairs does not last forever, the society decaying into mediocrity.

Departing Ollantaytambo, we drove to the high-altitude town of Pisac. Stepping off the bus, I expect to see Clint Eastwood in a poncho facing some bad guys; the white washed walls and cathedral fitting perfectly with his spaghetti westerns. The local market is even more from times gone by with authentic Peruvian clothes, including ponchos, for sale by people who undoubtedly had distant Inca relatives judging by their facial features, including deep tans and lines. I picked up some souvenirs happy to give these people the price they ask, that would be at least two-to-three times higher in Cusco. Aware that the altitude is not bothering me a bit, I realize that I'm fully acclimatized just in time to head back.

I spent a couple of days in the Miraflores area of Lima, leveling off. A visit to the Church of San Francisco and tour of the catacombs below it, containing the bones and skulls of many generations of priests, is an odd experience, highlighting how limited our time here is. On a more positive note, I actually got to view real Inca pieces at the Gold Museum. They were indeed masters of works both large and small.

An interesting experience occurred with my departure from Lima—The American Airlines flight was cancelled after a lengthy delay, forcing everyone to exit the departure gate with only one staff still working to stamp passports. By the time I made my way out to the check-in area, it was 2:33 AM, with over two hundred people lined up at one check-in kiosk. I felt sorry for the parents with crying children, but what can you do? The word spreading from the front of the line is that no American Airlines flights are available for a couple of days. At 6:00 AM after moving perhaps 20 people forward in the line, I shifted to the just opened Copa Airlines counter. There the helpful agent booked me on the 8:00 AM flight to Miami. Glad to leave the ridiculous scenario at the airport, and sad to leave Peru, I boarded the Copa Airlines flight. Once in Miami I knew I had to rebook my Air Canada flight to Toronto, from where I was to board a connecter flight to the next stop on my exploration of religions. The insurance compensation for the screw up in Peru could wait. Tired and relieved that I had solved a significant problem by shifting to Copa Airlines, I slept soundly dreaming about life in Inca times.

ANISHINAABE AND OBJIBWE RELGION

Thunder Bay is situated on the northern shore of Lake Superior, or Gitchigumi meaning Great Water or Great Lake, in Ontario, Canada. While the town has its picturesque aspects, of greater appeal is the largest lake in the world, containing an eighth of the freshwater on the planet. The lake is so large that it generates its own weather system, that at times of the year include sudden violent storms producing waves up to forty feet in height! Many boats, small and large, have met their ending when as the famous singer and songwriter, Gordon Lightfoot, wrote, "The lake, it is said, never gives up her dead when the skies of November turn gloomy." He put these words in the haunting song, The Wreck of the Edmund Fitzgerald, dedicated to the entire crew of 29 that perished on November 10, 1975, when a massive storm broke the huge boat in half!

Looking at the calm waters from the shore of Thunder Bay, it is difficult to imagine a monster storm, but history confirms many of them. At least equally impressive as these storms is what is arguably the most unique natural site in the world: The Sleeping Giant, a rock formation central to the Objibwe belief system. Amazingly, the peninsula that creates the bay of Thunder Bay, is shaped like a sleeping giant, the likeness being so striking that you'd swear someone or something carved it. The giant is on his back, with head, neck, massive chest and arms folded over it, body and legs, all clearly visible. Anyone with even the slightest spiritual inclination can only attribute this to a deity, or perhaps multiple deities.

At the tourism office by the shore, I booked an Objibwe guide, a young man who gave his name as Binesi, meaning thunderbird. We stood side-by side on the shore admiring the Sleeping Giant.

"No matter how many times you look, it always impresses."

"Yes, you don't see that every day for sure. Unless of course you live in Thunder Bay."

Smiling at my humor, he replied, "It gets pretty damn cold here in winter, and some people, even Objibwe, like to stay inside."

"It's fortunate that I'm visiting in the early autumn."

"For those who are active, and not too bothered by the cold, there's a great deal to do here in the winter, such as snowmobiling, or as most call it, sledding, snowshoe treks, ice fishing, and cross-country skiing. There's even downhill skiing. I do it all except for downhill skiing. This is a great place for outdoor activities, like with kayaking or canoeing in the warmer weather. I'll be taking you kayaking to see some pictograms made by my ancestors."

"Can we go over to the Sleeping Giant?"

"Ah, why would you want to see that little thing?"

Going with my young guide's humor I retorted, "True, I'll wait to see the really large rock formations."

"The Sleeping Giant is the largest realistic looking rock formation in the world. Sure, you can read images into almost anything, but this one doesn't require any reading, it's simply there!"

"You're right, I've seen many things in my travels, but can't recall any natural structure that even comes close. It must have had great meaning to your people."

"Sleeping Giant has profound significance for First Nations people of the region. Are you ready for some information?"

"Always ready for learning."

"Okay then, we'll start with the Anishinaabe related peoples. The Objibwe, Chippewa, Saulteaux, and Mississaugas are one group, another being the Algonquin and Nipissing. Then there are the Odawa, Potawatomi, and Oji-Cree as distinct groups, although we all are Anishinaabe, located mostly around the Great Lakes in Canada and the United States. According to stories passed on verbally, and also written on birch bark scrolls, our common distant ancestors lived on what has been called, Great Salt Water, almost for sure the Atlantic Ocean near the Gulf of St. Lawrence. In some versions, the origin is "Turtle Island" in the same region, related to how the Earth was to them the back of a turtle."

"That's an interesting notion, a turtle shell being rough with hills and valleys of sorts, so I can see how that idea could arise."

"They were trying to understand their world, like we all do, and derived meaning from the physical world. For some reason, the

Anishinaabe decided to migrate west. There are different stories that might explain it, most involving seven great miigis, which were said to be radiant beings in human form that appeared to people in the Waabanakiing, or Land of the Dawn. These miigis taught the Anishinaabe the ways of Midewiwin, with the teaching including following a miigis shell, or whiteshell, to the west, until they reached a place where food grows on water, this being wild rice. The migration began around 950 AD, and along the way some people decided to stay in a given area, while others continued on, resulting in the various Anishinaabe, related by genetics, language, and several cultural aspects. Of course, the groups diverged based on how they developed in the region they lived in."

"Interesting, I've heard most of the First Nations names you mentioned, but never understood the connection. Based on what you're saying the Objibwe settled in this region."

"That's right, and can you imagine coming upon this great lake; it must have been a clear sign to stay put. Then there is the legend of the Sleeping Giant, but you probably don't want to hear about it."

Smiling I retorted, "You're right, maybe instead tell me the story of how the first Tim Hortons coffee shop came to be in Thunder Bay."

Rolling with my humor, Binesi explained, "The great God of Lake Superior had trouble waking up, and declared that he needed coffee to start his day, and magically a Tim Hortons appeared the next day."

"Okay, now that the really interesting story has been told, you can bore me with the legend of the Sleeping Giant."

"The legend starts with Nanabijou, the Spirit of the Deep Sea Water, very important considering how deep Lake Superior is. Given the loyalty that the Objibwe people, living on what is now known as Isle Royale, showed to Nanabijou, and their peaceful and prosperous way of life, he decided to reward them. He summoned their Chief to his great Thunder Temple on a mountain, where he told a secret that if released to white men would result in him turning to stone. Clearly the legend must have been created later in our history, because white men were not around for a while. After the Chief made his promise, Nanabijou told of a rich silver mine, now known as Silver Islet. Nanabijou told the Chief to go to the highest point on Thunder Cape to find the entrance leading to the center of the mine.

Shortly, the Objibwe people became renowned for their beautiful silver ornaments, and when Sioux warriors captured wounded Objibwe warriors, they tortured them to learn the source of the mine, but none would reveal it. The Sioux then devised a trick, the notion of trickery being important to Anishinaabe peoples. A Sioux scout disguised himself and entered the Objibwe camp, where he soon learned the location of the mine. Sneaking off to the mine at night, he took some silver to prove he had succeeded. On the way to the Sioux camp, he traded the silver to white men, fur trappers, for food. The white men tricked the Sioux scout using alcohol, and he was persuaded to take them to the mine. Just when they were nearing Silver Islet, a monster storm broke out. The white men were drowned and the Sioux scout left in a crazed condition drifting aimlessly in his canoe. Of greater importance, the once open bay, was now filled by the Sleeping Giant, Nanabijou turned to stone."

"That's quite the story, and I have to say, much more interesting, although less humorous, than your story of the first Tim Hortons coffee shop in Thunder Bay."

"Now that you've heard the story, are you ready for a hike up it?"

"Yes, I've got my backpack with food and water, and sunscreen if needed."

"Good, then we'll drive over to the trailhead, and from there it's quite a hike."

The first section, the Kayebun Trail, although not steep is quite long, before connecting with the Talus Lake Trail. A short distance along the second trail we reached the Top of the Giant Trail, and began the steep ascent. When the trail leveled off we encountered a Top of the Giant sign by a creek and bench. An obvious and great place for a break, we relaxed and ate lunch.

"Once we're finished there's one more trail, much flatter, that will take us to the best view of Lake Superior you'll ever see."

Excited by the prospect I quickly finished my sandwich and off we went. Along the route Binesi pointed out various plants and birds from their calls. He explained, "The Objibwe and Anishinaabe generally live connected to nature, including the rocks, trees, plants, sun, moon, and water. We don't separate ourselves from them, but younger people seem more connected to electronic devices, unfortunately." His expression conveyed sadness. "Everything has a spirit, some like the rocks older, and others younger. When an animal is hunted we give thanks, believing that if we don't the spirits of that type of animal will no longer make themselves available."

"What about people spirits?"

"Yes, after death people continue on as spirits that help us, and we can communicate with them through various means, such as dreams and ceremonies. Dreams are seen as a way of gaining insight and knowledge of what will come, and are aided by ceremonies involving fasting and sweat lodges. In a traditional sweat lodge, water is pored over hot rocks in the center of a tent, and the heat and steam induces a dreamlike state. Undoubtedly, you've heard of dream catchers with the mesh and feathers that people put out to catch dreams at night."

"Yes, I've heard of them and noted some in the souvenir shop."

"Ah, the made in China ones."

"Like the fake bear claws."

"Capitalism applied to spirituality, very sad. Traditionally, a bear claw symbolizes healing. To obtain a bear claw is difficult, and the wearer is accorded respect and honor. An eagle feather symbolizes strength, and brings respect as well, it also being difficult to acquire."

"I've heard that plants had, or have, roles too."

"Very definitely. Tobacco for instance is an important part of ceremonies, and symbolizes honesty. In the past it was often a mixture of tobacco and other plants, such as dogwood and bearberry. The smoke is thought to lift prayers to the creator God, Gitchi-Manitou. In ceremonies tobacco represents the east. White sage the west, and this plant is used to purify. White cedar symbolizes the south, while sweet grass represents the north. The strands of sweet grass are thought to be the hair of Ogashiinan, or Mother-Earth. You see how everything in nature has a role and is connected."

"Including the Sleeping Giant." My comment came as we reached the end of the trail. Proceeding slowly Binesi led me out onto rock towers.

"Please be very careful of your step and do not go close to the edge, or you will become part of the Sleeping Giant."

Normally not bothered by heights, I felt a little giddy perched on the edge of a vertical rock tower, looking down almost 1,000 ft. at the surface of Lake Superior. Raising my gaze, I took in the panoramic view of the bay, land, and lake. Consistent with it being the largest freshwater lake in world, the deep blue surface stretches to infinity. "I can imagine that your ancestors must have seen this as the center of the universe. I mean the Sleeping Giant, the view from here, and the massive lake."

"It is powerful, for sure."

"At night a person must feel that they can almost touch the heavens!"

"Now you're getting the spirit, excuse the pun."

"I know you're joking, but I get the idea of everything imbued with a spirit, and connected. This is something that cultures very reliant on nature seem to believe. When civilizations grow and people are less directly reliant on nature, their religious views disconnect from the natural world."

"Good insight. Tomorrow we're going to kayak to pictograms that will probably strengthen your notion. Now, though, we should head back as the sun sets earlier in autumn and the trail is much harder in the dark."

On the way back, Binesi explained the challenges he experiences keeping in tune with the ancient ways. As with so much of the world, You Tube videos are taking over, and few young people seem to care, unless Objibwe ways appear on a You Tube video. He described how the forest surrounding Lake Superior offers an abundance of food, such as fiddleheads, berries, and mushrooms, and also meat in winter, but everyone wants corporation made food shipped from the south. As such they are all now reliant on "just on time delivery," when a virtually unlimited and largely free grocery store lies next door in nature! Growing up in a populated area, the concept of food being available without a visit to a grocery store seems very intriguing. It certainly ties First Nations peoples to the natural world, and that link in turn, is very important to their religious belief system.

The next day brought with it the luck of calm water. In a kayak, I did not feel like braving massive waves or anything close to them. Fortunately, the sun is shining bright, it's light penetrating the surface of Lake Superior, highlighting the smooth rocks, some the size of cars and even larger, near the shore.

Noting my gaze directed below the surface, Binesi explained, "This is the Canadian Shield, rock exposed when glaciers retreated some 10,000 years ago. They stripped off much of the soil, and also carved out many of the lakes, although I read that Lake Superior formed much earlier when the continental plate almost broke apart, creating a rift. That's why it's so large and deep."

As we approached a flat cliff face, he stopped his kayak. "What do you see?"

At first just the steep cliff face, but then a diagram on the rock. "Up there, a creature of some sort drawn."

"Yes, it is Mishi Peshu or Mishipashoo, spellings vary as with so many things in Anishinaabeg culture. You're looking at the great underwater lynx, who lives in the depths of Gitchigumi. Forbidding, isn't he?"

"A tail and back with razor spikes, and horns on his head. I'll say he's forbidding."

"His body is like a sea serpent, but this is not as obvious as the other features. Mishi Peshu symbolizes the mystery, dangers, and power of the lake he resides in. To ensure a safe passage my ancestors offered tobacco along with prayers. Failure to do so could result in a massive storm and death."

"I imagine that this wall must be pounded by waves during those storms, so how does this drawing survive?"

"They used red ochre, a pigment made from iron ore and mixed with clay. It stands the test of time, or perhaps the spirit of Mishu Peshu ensures that it does." His last statement was made with a smile and twinkle in his eye.

For the next few hours we paddled around exploring the shoreline, landing at a few pebbly beaches, and having lunch on a sun baked rock, nice and warm to the touch, while watching the sun dance on the wave caps. Braving the cool water, I dove in swimming underwater. Opening my eyes, I'm mesmerized by the sun rays tracing unique patterns on the smooth rocks beneath the surface, and for a moment believe that I can make out the image of the great underwater lynx. Yes, I'm into the spirit, and feel sad at the prospect of leaving such an inspirational site, and a natural one at that.

We spent the remainder of the day paddling by more cliff faces, some with pictograms of animals, including water snakes, and people in canoes. We also visited small islets, many only containing a few evergreen trees. I wonder if the spirits of Binesi's ancestors are watching our passage. It's an interesting notion, how we all might continue on as spirits that reside in nature, instead of destined for some heaven or hell. Actually, from my experience of Lake Superior this is likely heaven, at least in the warm and calm weather. Maybe it's hell in the stormy and cold weather, who knows?

Following my Lake Superior experience learning about the Objibwe and Anishinaabe more generally, I returned to my world of medical practice knowing it will take several months to save up for my next and last excursion—The exploration of Eastern religions. Eager to see me, and me to see her, Aminta visited for a week. I took a few days off devoting it to developing our relationship, that transformed into a romance during the visit. It definitely appears that we will be seeing more of each other in the not too distant future, but my focus now is on rounding out my knowledge of world religions with information about Hinduism and Buddhism.

HINDUISM

Varanasi India was described by Mark Twain as "Older than history, older than tradition, older even than legend, and looks twice as old as all of them put together." It is one of the holiest of cities to Hindus, and one of the oldest continually inhabited cities on the planet. However, for such an old city it has the vibrancy of youth, with a palpable energy running through it. Reading about how difficult it can be to navigate the city, and certainly while trying to learn about Hinduism, I opted to book a package well in advance, with a pickup at the airport, transfer to the hotel, and guided tours. A very neatly dressed, thin, middle-aged man met me upon arrival.

He spoke in thickly accented, but very proper, English, "I am Arjun, your guide. I will escort you to a taxi that will take us to your hotel for your stay. Since it is morning we will start the tour, if that pleases you."

"Yes, it does very much, as I slept well on the flight, and I'm looking forward to seeing the sites." Deciding to check if Arjun is well versed in Hinduism, I asked, "I understand that you're quite knowledgeable about Hinduism?"

"Yes sir, I am Hindu, as are 80% of people in India, and I have also studied it well, although you will be the judge of my knowledge."

"Sounds perfect, let's start the experience."

The drive to the hotel brought to mind my arrival in Cairo that now seems so long ago. Traffic, traffic, and more traffic, but at least in Cairo there seems to be space for it to somehow move. In Varanasi there is at least as much traffic as Cairo, but no space for it to move, although move it does suggesting the assistance of some Hindu God or Goddess. Given the close proximity of vehicles and vehicles, and vehicles and pedestrians, I figure that insurance must be near impossible to get, or the rates prohibitive. Driving requires constant attention, and even the obviously experienced taxi driver minimized talking. As expected, we arrived too early for my room, so I quickly changed into more comfortable clothes before having the bags placed in storage.

While still in the pleasingly spacious and air-conditioned hotel lobby, Arjun explained, "As you have seen, Varanasi is a very crowded city, and you will probably be shocked, or at least surprised, by what you will see. I say this because some visitors are not prepared for a different world, and Varanasi is very unique, even for India."

"Thanks for the warning, but I'm quite well travelled."

"Yes, I think you'll be fine."

As we squeezed into narrow alleyways packed with people, I started to feel a sense of dread, almost claustrophobia. Maybe it was having my wallet stolen in the crowd at Athens airport, but I placed my valuables in the hotel safe prior to the current tour. Perhaps it was the failed suicide bomber in Rome, or maybe just the density of people you'd only expect at a rock concert, although such a venue is much more open. Just as I began to get that panicky feeling like I have to escape, the world opened up to a view of the Ganges River with a very blue sky framing it. Over to our right side by the water, I noted smoke and a group of people. Curious I asked, "What's going on there."

Smiling my guide expressed, "This is one of the things tourists are not prepared for. Let's walk over but keep to the building side." Arriving at an alleyway perpendicular to the river scene he stopped. "We will wait a few minutes."

A distant and distorted chanting reached my ears, low at first but building. An image came to mind from The Mummy movie, with a crowd chanting "Imhotep," however, as the sound grew I realized this is something much different. When the chanting peaked, a stretcher of sorts carried by six men emerged, trailing a chanting crowd. Seeing the figure on the stretcher covered in gold-colored cloth, I suddenly realized that this is not a medical emergency but a funeral procession. Hanging back by the building we watched as the procession passed across a flat section of the riverfront, then down some stairs to the water. Too surprised, or shocked, to say anything, I observed as the bearers placed the body on the ground, at which point a chanting person sprinkled river water over it. If this is not unique enough, the pallbearers then raised the deceased and placed him or her on a large stack of wood, set up like a bonfire. I knew what would come next but found myself disbelieving it, until a man dressed in robes came down from the concrete walkway with a container holding a flame. He applied it to the wood below the deceased and in no time the person literally went up in smoke. The chanters continued their words, as they pulled back from the smoke and flames.

Gathering my composure, I expressed, "You don't see that every day."

"You do if you live or visit here each day. These funerals can go on all day and night!"

"You're joking."

"No sir, I never joke about such matters."

"But why, what's the purpose?"

"In the Hindu religion, the Ganges is a very sacred river, and the Varanasi section particularly so. The steps leading to the river are called ghats, and some are set out for funerals. People from all over India bring their dead here to first be purified with water from the Ganges, and then cremated. Hinduism maintains that people and animals are reincarnated, potentially millions of times. Cremation frees the soul for another rebirth. A part of the skull, the foramen, is opened to allow the soul to exit. Being cremated in this holy location also allows a person to escape the cycles of birth and death, and have their soul rest, assuming that the person has achieved what is called moksha."

"What does that mean?"

"It is a high level of the soul, sufficient to free it from rebirths. Basically, there are three main ways that moksha is achieved, known as marga, or the Way. The first is the way of knowledge or insight, jnana. The second is bhakti, the way of devotion. The third is karma, the way of action."

"I've heard of karma, but what is it exactly?"

"Karma is a moral law present in the universe, like gravity. The degree of good or bad karma influences rebirth, and a person acquires good karma by leading a moral life."

"Do Hindu people really try and adhere to this."

"Most do, but as everywhere there are those who accumulate bad karma through deceit and treachery."

"It is human nature."

"Unfortunately, yes. Hinduism, though, does show compassion, and it is understood that a person cannot fulfill all three components of marga in a single life."

"How does it work with reincarnation, after the soul leaves a body?"

"The soul reaches Yama, Lord of the Dead, who reviews a person's deeds and decides the level of reincarnation."

"So, there is no heaven or hell?"

"The form of reincarnation can be seen as different levels of heaven and hell. Good karma leads to a good reincarnation, so it is basically heaven."

"Then why do people strive for moksha and freedom from rebirths?"

"You are very inquisitive, and certainly one of the most interested persons I have provided a tour for, which pleases me. The level of your questions challenge, as we are getting into the realm of very conceptual Hinduism. However, I will endeavor to answer your enlightened questions in your quest for jnana."

Considering his last comment, I had to agree that is what I'm doing, "Yes, I suppose I am seeking jnana."

"You are on your way to a good rebirth then, and even more so if your karma is good, which I think is the case."

"I try and do good."

"Getting back to your complicated question, there is a hierarchical aspect to Hinduism, that some believe provides for our caste system. Through rebirths a person can achieve higher levels for their soul, and if moksha based on the three paths is sufficient, then the soul has achieved a sufficient level and can rest. At this point a person can be free of the birth-death-rebirth cycles."

"That's an excellent explanation, and I can see how these beliefs might influence your caste system. I've noted that there always seems to be a hierarchical aspect to religions in one or more ways, such as different levels of Gods and Goddesses, a single all powerful God above people, or different statuses in the religion itself."

"Yes, hierarchies do characterize people, and I will now show you an example." Pointing towards the edge of the cremation ghat, he asked, "You see the piles of ashes by the water?"

Peering through the smoke I can just make out a large pile. "Yes, it's quite a collection."

"Keepers, who are of a lower status, will push ashes of the deceased into the water when enough accumulate."

"That's quite the job."

"Even more unique is how they will often use metal poles to ensure that unburned limbs are fully cremated. If you are from a poor family, the quality and quantity of wood might not lead to a full cremation. The wealthy import fine wood from other areas, and enough to ensure a complete cremation, reducing the keeper's work. Lowest status, co called "untouchables" will sift the ashes for bits of gold or other precious metals, to be used to help the poor pay for sufficient wood."

"Yes, very different statuses in this and the afterworld." Considering the sights at the cremation ghat, I added, "I now appreciate your mentioning at the hotel how tourists are often not prepared. This is very different from anything I've seen."

"Let us walk along." As we began our stroll down the waterfront, I heard chants again starting somewhere back along the alleyway. Looking over my shoulder I watched another body emerge as the chants reached a crescendo. It's difficult to imagine this going on all day and night, but that's what it is.

Stopping by a ghat further along lacking funeral pyres, Arjun asked, "What do you see happening here?"

The scene before me, although crowded with people, seemed much more upbeat, people bathing while mostly dressed. Recalling the purification with water at the funeral ghat, I suggested, "They're probably purifying themselves with water from the Ganges."

"Exactly, many people come to wash away their sins and bad karma here. The river Goddess Ganga is worshipped, and according to Hinduism, the river initially only flowed in the heavens. A sage, Bhagiratha, using his great karma convinced the Gods to allow it to flow to Earth. One of our greatest Gods, Shiva, that Varanasi is mostly devoted to, broke Ganga's fall to Earth by catching her in his hair, and they have been consorts ever since, despite Shiva being married to Parvati."

"You've drawn an interesting image, with a river flowing from the heavens to where we are, and in such a fashion."

"There are many interesting stories in the Hindu religion, which is one of the reasons it's the third most popular religion in the world, after Christianity and Islam."

"What else do you think makes it so popular?"

"There is the age of the religion, as it dates to around 2,500 BC, with traditions of the Dravidian and Aryan cultures the beginnings. About 1,500 BC the Aryans invaded the northwestern India region bringing oral texts called Vedas, which are considered eternal truths, and the basis of Hinduism. They have been written down in this the age of Kali Yuga, or degeneration: Hinduism maintains that there are cycles of time, and no origin, so my description of the origins of our religion actually does not hold any meaning to most Hindus. According to the Vedic religion there are many elemental Gods and Goddesses. From these arose within Hinduism the trimurti, or trinity, of Brahma, Vishnu, and Shiva. Perhaps to include the features of the many Gods and Goddess, these three have several interpretations."

"That must get very confusing."

"It can, but it also makes the deities appealing to everyone, as there are many meanings, another reason why Hinduism is so popular. In addition, we believe that all reality is one, so different beliefs and entities like people, animals, the sun, and moon, merge."

"I suppose that the notion of repeat lives also makes the religion popular."

"To a certain extent, but what you will be reborn as might not be that appealing, and many lives can be tiring, leading some to want to escape the cycle, favoring the cremations here."

"In my exploration of religions, I haven't encountered one where three Gods and Goddesses stand out."

"Hinduism is unique, and even more given that only one deity can have meaning to a person or group. Some worship just Shiva, Vishnu, or Brahma, while others worship multiple deities."

"So even though it is a multiple deity belief system, it can be interpreted as a single God?"

"Perhaps, but a feature of Hinduism is flexibility and inclusion of many beliefs, so it is not a single God system."

"I'm curious about the different interpretations or faces of the Gods and Goddesses."

"Let us consider Shiva. In the Shiva Purana text he is everything, appearing in many forms, and having over a thousand names!"

"Quite the God."

"Yes, and this repeats for at least Vishnu." Removing a notebook from his pocket he turned to a page with several small diagrams. "These are the different forms of Shiva." Pointing in turn he explained, "There is Mahakala Lord of Time, Maheshvara Lord of Knowledge, and Bhairava the Destroyer. Shiva can be represented as male or female, peaceful or angry, and the like. We believe that those who die in Varanasi go straight to Shiva, even if they have bad karma."

I found myself drawn to the picture of Shiva as the Destroyer, with a ring of fire, his right foot on a small person, and left on the ring. It appears that he has four arms, two holding something, and hair extending out almost touching the ring of fire. "That's a powerful image."

Turning to a page devoted entirely to it, Arjun explained, "I will indicate some unique features. Shiva's right foot is on a dwarf demon representing ignorance. He has a third eye symbolizing higher consciousness but that can also unleash fire, and Ganga is on a strand of hair here to the right; recall the story of how Shiva saved Ganga's fall from the heavens." Pointing to two hands he added, "Of particular significance is what he holds in these two hands: In the left is the flame of destruction, and the right is a double-sided drum representing rebirth. Shiva is the God of destruction and also rebirth, as the diagram symbolizes.

Hinduism maintains that there are three fundamental states of the cosmos: Evolution, or development, existence, and involution, acting as a cyclic process. Each of the three main deities control one of these processes. Brahma as the creator is responsible for evolution, although not in the scientific sense. Vishnu is the preserver of existence, and Shiva who was last to complete the cycle, responsible for involution and then rebirth.

Our next stop—Kashi Viswanath Temple—one of our finest and most sacred temples is going to show you something very powerful pertaining to the three states of the cosmos. Normally, non-Hindus are not allowed in, and I would not attempt to do so for most, but you are very devoted to jnana, and such an entrance will help. I am well known to the guards and temple keepers and we can quickly visit, but keep this to yourself. Are you ready for some walking as it's further along the Ganges?"

"Love to walk, and thanks for the unique opportunity!"

Looking up at the three golden spires topping Kashi Viswanath Temple, I immediately appreciate the importance. The two tall spires ascend in levels of smaller spires and numerous ornate carvings, while the central smaller spire curves in before rising to a point. Such an elaborate temple could only be for a major God or Goddess.

As if reading my mind, Arjun stated, "A temple fit for Shiva, no?"

"I'll say, but why is it named without mentioning Shiva?"

"Recall when I said that Shiva has many names?" Without waiting for a reply, he continued, "Shiva is also known as Vishwanath or Ruler of the Universe, and Kashi is another name for the city."

"It might take a while getting used to all the names for the same God or place."

"To visitors yes, but we grow up with this complexity. In the case of this temple everyone knows that it is one of the holiest sites in India, being the main temple to Shiva."

After conversing quietly with a couple of guards, and then temple keepers, Arjun led me to a small inner courtyard with alternating dark and light floor tiles, columns, and massive bells hanging down. Two men wearing robs, sat facing each other on benches. "The bells are to ward off evil spirits during worship. Temples vary but a key aspect is the representation of the three fundamental states of the cosmos. This is what I want you to see, as it is one of the holiest Hindu symbols, and the most holy here."

After leading me to a silver box on the floor containing an odd shaped structure, comprised of an elongated piece extending horizontally from a circular base, and a dark stone pointed up like a rod, he continued, "This is the Shiva lingam, the central icon in all his temples. Brahma as the creator is represented by the base for evolution, Vishnu the preserver the long flat section for existence, and Shiva the destroyer the top rod for involution. The rod can be interpreted as Shiva's phallus for generative power." No humor evident in his delivery. "During various ceremonies, the top rod for Shiva is decorated and worshipers celebrate." Pulling out his notebook he showed me a picture of the room crowded with robbed men, and flowers adorning the rod section. "You are fortunate to see such a holy icon in such a holy site."

Back in the sunlight, or what filtered into the alley, I thought about the Hindu notion of cycles and associated deities. Realizing that I know next to nothing about the other two main deities I commented, "Even though I'm aware that Brahma is the creator and Vishnu the preserver, I don't have any real understanding of them."

"And you like to understand." His words carried a tone of certainty. He turned to a page of his notebook showing an androgynous figure wearing a blue garment with many symbols, a gold cloth hanging from the shoulders or neck, and curly blondish hair. This time four arms are unmistakable, the top right with a circular object, top left a conch shell, the bottom left a lotus flower, and the bottom right a ball-like object on a string. "This is of a painting showing Vishnu as the universe with all the forces present within him. What features stand out?"

"Other than the colors, the objects in his hands." I felt relieved that Arjun defined the sex of Vishnu as I was not at all certain from the painting. However, if Vishnu is like Shiva, he can be represented different ways.

"That is what most people identify. The disk in his upper right hand symbolizes the mind and the sun, and the combination universal domination. The golden mace in his lower right hand is for primeval knowledge and the power of the mind, in particular authority and maintaining order. The conch shell in his upper left hand is for the primordial vibration from creation, "Om," that is blown at temples to indicate the presence of Vishnu. The water lotus in his lower left hand signifies universal purity and fertility."

"Why does he and also Shiva have four arms?"

"They symbolize the directions of space—North, south, east, and west."

"That makes sense. How about the images on," I hesitated as I wanted to say dress, "on the whatever he's wearing?"

"They depict the various forms of Vishnu and other Gods. The overall image embodies many Hindu Gods. Pointing to a dark man on a horse located on Vishnu's lower left arm he explained, "This is Yama, Lord of the Dead. The images on Vishnu's arms are all of vasus, eight Gods of the elements. On the upper right arm there is Ishana vasu of the northeast, and Kubera vasu of the north. The images on Vishnu's lower right arm are vasu's of the wind, Vayu, and waters, Varuna. On his upper left arm are Indra vasu of the east, and Agni vasu of fire. The lower left has Yama, as I mentioned, and also Nirriti vasu of the southwest."

Shifting my attention to Vishnus's legs he explained, "The seven tiers here represent the seven lower regions, or Patala, of the cosmos. For example, the snakes are images of Vasuki, the cobra and King of Snakes, ruling nether regions."

"So much information in one figure!"

"And then there are many little figures representing an overall concept." Turning to another page he showed me ten figures, each of a person standing or sitting, one on a horse. "These are the avatars, or in other words, incarnations of Vishnu, manifesting in the world to preserve it."

Looking at the images I found myself drawn to one consisting of a person on a turtle. "Who's this?"

"Kurma the turtle, who helped create the world by supporting it on his back."

The Anishinaabe symbolism of the world as the back of a turtle came to me, accounting for my interest in it. "I've seen that same type of image in North American First Nations belief systems."

"The turtle is solid and strong, so it could repeat in different cultures. I will show a couple of others you might recognize." Pointing to a figure seated cross legged he stated, "This is Buddha, the enlightened one, someone you might identify with." A smile accompanied his comment. "Then there is Krishna, that you will recall from the Hare Krishna movement." He indicated a standing figure holding a rod, smaller than the rest.

"Your major deities do seem to cover virtually all aspects of the universe, don't they?"

"They do not miss much."

"What about Brahma?"

"Brahma is not as popular as Shiva and Vishnu, but is very important." Turning to another page Arjun revealed a four-headed and four-arm figure seated with legs crossed. "This is Brahma, the four heads and also arms indicating directions. As with the other two Gods, what is held in his hands is very important, all symbols of knowledge and creation. There are the sacred texts of Vedas, rosary beads symbolizing time, a ladle for fire, and a water pot signifying water of course, all necessary for creation. He wears a crown in this and other depictions."

"Why is he less famous than the others?"

"I do not exactly know, but it might be that he is the creator, and this was done before the present. Vishnu preserves what we all know, and Shiva is the one who will end it for another cycle. Their roles might seem more relevant now to most. Brahma has few temples devoted to him, only really Pushkar in Rajasthan."

"I think he needs a public relations agency to help out."

"That is certainly a worthwhile idea. It might help you to understand that even though Hindus have many temples, although not for Brahma, temples are not central to our worship. Icons that are believed to contain and represent the deity are worshipped mainly in the house. Worship consists of mantras, or vibrating sounds that summon the deity, and prasad, the offering of gifts, that in earlier times consisted of sacrifices. The main role of worship is offering of the self to become one with the deity, and darshan, meaning seeing and being in the presence of the icon, is how this is achieved. Even in the temples, the icon is most important; recall the lingam you saw."

"So why even have temples?"

"That is a good question. In some ways they are for promotion, or your PR, in others they house an important historic icon to the deity."

"Maybe Brahma doesn't need the publicity, since he's the creator."

"That could well be."

At this point we emerged on a major street judging by the width and traffic. Arjun escorted, or more accurately, guided, me back to the hotel. Based upon our time together we clearly resonated with each other, due to what might best be described as polite intellectualism.

That evening around sunset he took me to a nearby house of friends, where I was treated to an authentic Indian meal, activating all mouth sensations possible. At sunset, prior to the meal, I quietly witnessed the couple worshipping Shiva. A small section of the living room wall, with a gold colored background, was the focal point. It contained a small statue that I took to be a Shiva icon, with flowers and water to the sides. The experience gave a very personal touch to the information acquired about Hinduism.

The next day was spent seeing more temples with Arjun, but nothing compared to that first day, and if not for our pleasant and informative discussion about more detailed aspects of Hinduism and life in India, I could easily have skipped it. It was harder moving on from Arjun than most of the other guides I'd encountered, but the journey of discovery had become my mission.

BUDDHISM

From the patient response of drivers in Bangkok, I sense that Buddhism must teach the value of patience. In Cairo nothing, not even traffic lights stop the traffic, in Varanasi it somehow moves often in incredibly narrow streets, but in Bangkok the traffic simply stops dead, and yet there is almost no honking of horns, no single finger salutes, no shouted obscenities. Very un-North American indeed. It seems that I could have walked faster from the airport to the hotel along the Chao Phraya River, but then the stifling heat would have slowed me down, and it is a long way. Settling into my modern ninth floor room, overlooking the river that has been described as the "Venice of the East," I lay back on the bed and dozed out. Sometimes travel just catches up to a person, and you have to catch up on rest.

Waking refreshed at just after 3:00 o'clock in the afternoon, I made my way to the outdoor pool, grabbed a towel and one of the few available lounge chairs, sat back, and did more relaxing. Normally I'm a high-energy person, both physically and mentally, just not today. Looking around at the other tourists, being careful not to stare, I tried to imagine what it would be like just vacationing by a pool or beach, with no tours. Other than admiring the near naked bathing suit beauties, it would be pretty boring after a day or two. It's hard to explain, but I usually feel more rested and relaxed when I'm active, assuming the activity is stimulating.

A nice tropical cocktail with colors matching that of the setting sun, settled me even more. As day shifted to night I shifted off the chair, briefly returning to my room to prepare for dinner. Gazing out the window at the river and lights across the shore, particularly those cast on a tall temple, I realize that Bangkok actually does have some of the best, and certainly most accessible, Buddhist temples.

Following dinner at the hotel restaurant adorned with bamboo walls, and lighted fish ponds, I booked a couple of tours, this time with small groups. The first consisting of a land-based excursion to the Royal Palace and major temples, and then a river and canal cruise the following day. Satisfying my need for rest, I went to bed early.

The Royal Palace is really more a sprawling complex than a palace per se. A white wall with small defense towers at the corners and entrance gates along the sides, surrounds gold-capped buildings. Approaching in our mini-van I had the impression we are arriving at an amusement park, due to how colorful and massive it looks from outside the perimeter wall. However, a roller coaster would be out of place, as I discovered once inside. On this tour, and as it turned out the next day as well, I have two guides, one a young woman, Fah, and the other a young man, Gan. Fah explained on the drive that Gan is in training, and he is now doing the on the job part. Hopefully, two guides are better than one. I will soon find out.

Fah started the tour off by announcing, "Gan will be giving us a presentation as we walk from here, the outer courtyard, to the middle courtyard. I will fill in if additional information is needed."

Clearing his throat Gan began somewhat formally, "This whole complex is the Royal Palace. It consists of different sections including the outer courtyard we are in now, mostly with government buildings, the middle courtyard, the inner courtyard, and the Temple of the Emerald Buddha. I, I mean we, will now take you to the middle courtyard."

Silence followed as he led us through a gate to an incredibly symmetrical and distinct building, with golden spires on both sides of the roof, plus one rising from the middle of a central rectangular extension. Just below the roof, arches extend right across the front. Gan's voice intruded on my observations, "This is Phra Thinang Chakri Prasat, one of the most unique buildings because it blends traditional Thai and European architecture. The top has a Thai green and orange tiled roof, and also gilded spires known as prasats. The lower sections are clearly European in style. In 1875 King Rama V went to Singapore and Java, and brought back an English architect, John Clunich, and his assistant, to design and construct the throne hall that is on the lower level. The king wanted it all European." Attempting some humor, he hesitated before adding, "I guess he got bored with all this colorful Thai stuff." With only a few brief laughs, Gan went back to his presentation. "His Chief Minister was not happy with the prospect of an all European building and convinced him to add the top Thai part."

Piping in Fah stated, "And now the world has an amazing blend of the two styles." Directing Gan she added, "Gan, perhaps we can give them some background on Thai history and the Royal Palace."

"Certainly Fah. Thailand was initially known as Siam. The capital was across the Chao Phraya River at Thonburi. King Buddha Yodfa Chulaloke, known as Rama I, moved the capital here to Bangkok and had this temple started in 1782. It was the residence of the king and royal government until 1925. Major government events are still held here, but it is no longer a royal residence." As Gan led us around the complex explaining Thai history, I found myself drifting off to all sorts of thoughts and images, from Aminta to various events and sites I've seen on my quest. It was probably the relatively monotonous presentation by Gan, and certainly compared to the intellectual connection with Arjun in Varanasi, that triggered my daydreaming. It was only when we approached what obviously, at least to me, seemed to be a temple that I tuned in again.

"This is the Temple of the Emerald Buddha, or Wat Phra Kaew, one of the most revered in all of Thailand!"

Before he could continue, an elderly man in our group asked, "What are those spiky things extending from the top?"

"They are called chofa, or sky tassels, placed on wats, meaning temples, and royal buildings. A chofa looks like a tall thin bird, and is meant to resemble a mystical creature called Garuda, a half-man, half-bird vehicle of the Hindu God Vishnu."

This reference to Vishnu and Hinduism certainly snagged my attention, Vishnu the preserver needing avatars and other agents to assist in preserving the world. The chofa clearly demonstrates the connection between Hinduism and Buddhism.

"The columns support a gilded roof common to temples and royal buildings. The number of chofa on it also signify an important building." Addressing a more practical matter, Gan explained, "Entering the temple we must remove shoes, and have arms covered as mentioned prior to the tour. For those of you who missed this requirement we have shoulder and arm covers and socks, as bare feet cannot touch the temple."

Once inside I began looking for the Emerald Buddha, but it didn't seem to be present. I noticed others looking puzzled. Seeing our confusion, Fah quickly reacted explaining, "The Emerald Buddha is over there on that stand. It is only 26 inches, or 66 centimeters, tall, so easy to miss if you're looking for something large. It is not made of emeralds, but jade; for Thai's "emerald" means green. The story goes that lightning struck a wat in northern Thailand in 1434 revealing a small statue covered in stucco. Underneath this covering lay the Emerald Buddha, and it came to be revered as one of the primary images of Buddha. It represents Buddha in a meditating or yogic posture. The clothes are changed depending on the season. I guess even Buddha wants to be fashionable." Her timely and effortless comic delivery, compared to her less experienced colleague, produced a round of laughter. Going with the flow she added, "Although his fashions are not easy to find."

Thinking of how Hindu deities have different expressions, I mentioned, "It's like Hinduism where Gods and Goddesses can have many forms or expressions."

"Yes, exactly. Buddhism arose from Hinduism with Buddha being one of the avatars of Vishnu." Seeing puzzled looks, other than from me, she added, "Vishnu is one of the main Hindu Gods, and avatars are incarnations assisting him in the world. Buddhism started with Siddhartha Gautama, who lived in northeast India around the sixth to fourth century before Christ." Realizing that she had taken over the presentation from Gan, she glanced at him before stating, "I'll turn the rest of the talk over to my colleague."

Taking his cue and looking relieved that his supervisor gave him another chance, Gan explained with more enthusiasm than his prior monotone presentation, "Siddhartha Gautama was actually from a royal family, not what you would think of for such a humble person. It is said that his father tried to protect him from the evils of life by keeping him confined to the palace, but curious to see the world he went outside the palace on chariot rides. On different occasions, he witnessed a sick man, an old man, a corpse, and a wandering holy man. These four occurrences are known as the Four Signs, and they led Siddhartha Gautama to search for meaning in life. Based on seeing the wandering holy man, he decided to give up the life he knew, leaving his wife and family, and embarked on a homeless existence, referred to as the Great Renunciation."

"We'd call that mental illness back home." The comment arose from an elderly woman in the group.

Showing the capacity to think on his feet, Gan replied, "In most instances this would be so, but Siddhartha Gautama went on to create one of the world's most influential religions, something that a severely mentally ill person would not be successful at." Noting the woman's silent acceptance of his explanation he continued, "Feeling despair Siddhartha Gautama sought enlightenment and achieved it while meditating under a Bodhi tree in a deer park in Varanasi."

The name of that most unique city triggered memories of my recent visit, along with the mixture of feelings that it tends to produce. I commented, "I've just been to Varanasi, and I can see how it is a place that can lead to enlightenment."

Addressing my comment Gan replied, "Although I have never been so fortunate to visit it, I have heard it is unique and inspirational to those seeking answers. Siddhartha Gautama found answers there understanding the true nature of suffering, and from that point on he became the Buddha, meaning "the awoken one," and not the homeless person awoken by the authorities." This time his attempt at humor paid off producing a round of laughter. When the laughter subsided, he added, "Buddha went on to teach for forty or so years prior to his death."

"How did his ideas differ from Hinduism, since that was his starting point?" The mention of Varanasi tweaked my curiosity of how Buddhism diverged from Hinduism.

Demonstrating his knowledge Gan effortlessly explained, "Buddha accepted many of the Hindu beliefs, such as rebirth with many lives, and karma, but diverged with his belief that there is no soul, or atman, that is reborn. According to his teachings there is no permanence to anything, only a sequence of one moment of appearance leading to the next. He also believed that the goal is not union with a God, but nirvana, which is the blowing out of the fires of attachment and longing, or in other words achieving a detached state. Interestingly, it was the Hindu God Brahma who persuaded him to teach others what he had learned."

Noting a look from Fah, he shifted the focus, "Buddha has many expressions and representations, and we will shortly be seeing some others, but first we will finish our tour of the Royal Palace." As he led the way through the grounds he pointed out dome structures with tall points. "These are known as stupas, and contain the cremated remains of Buddhist monks or nuns. They are derived from a more ancient burial form where the body was placed sitting up."

As we continued our walk Gan explained, "Our next stop is truly amazing showing a reclining Buddha, and one slightly larger than the Emerald Buddha."

Dwarfed by the 150 feet (46 meter) gold Buddha reclining on his side, head propped up with his right hand, I appreciated Gan's now obviously humorous comment about a slightly larger imagine than the Emerald Buddha. I found myself appreciating how an insect must feel, if they feel, upon seeing a person. Perhaps this was the intent of the designers? The enormous size of the Reclining Buddha image is accentuated by the tightness of the surrounding building, leaving limited space to spare around the central figure.

After a few people uttered "Wow!" and "It's amazing!" Gan stated, "See I told you it's slightly larger than the Emerald Buddha, although only slightly. The whole temple complex is known as Wat Pho, and it houses more Buddha images than any other temple in Thailand. Obviously, this is the star attraction. The core is brick covered by modelled plaster, and capped in gold leaf. Please don't consider trying to take it, though, as everyone's pockets will be searched on the way out." He definitely had hit his comedic stride and comfort zone of the presentation.

After a shy and tense start, I began to think that Gan might best be suited for a career in standup comedy. Adding to the humor I suggested, "Maybe we can back the van up and take it."

The lightness of our humorous comments proved infectious, and everyone in the group appeared more relaxed than at the Royal Palace, even though it is only a ten-minute walk away. Continuing with his presentation Gan explained, "Buddha's head is resting on two box pillows encrusted with glass mosaic tiles." Walking the full length to the feet he added, "His soles are three meters high, and divided into 108 panels. This number represents the positive actions and symbols Buddha applied to achieve nirvana. There are also the same number of bowls along the corridor we just covered, for donations if anyone wishes to do so. Meritorious acts, such as giving to monks, helps ensure a good rebirth."

"What acts work against a good rebirth?" A young man silent and seemingly bored until this point of the presentation, asked the question.

"There are three cardinal faults of humanity: Greed represented by a pig, hatred symbolized by a snake, and delusion blinding a person to the truth, as a rooster. Buddhism represents the cosmos in circular terms to stress the notion of cyclical processes, and the Wheel of Life contains the three cardinal faults at the center. Surrounding these faults are the six spheres of existence: Gods, Asuras or rebel Gods, hungry ghosts resulting from greed, hell, the beasts or in other words animals, and humans. The human sphere is very important, because it is the only one where your behavior and so outcome can be controlled. Suffering in this realm arises from egoism, ignorance, and desire. A central belief that Buddha gave to the world, is that by detaching yourself from these actions you can achieve nirvana and freedom from the cycles of births and rebirths."

"That all sounds pretty complicated, compared to just God." The young man had found his voice expressing a preference for monotheism.

"It is complicated, as Hindu and Buddhism involve many components and expressions, mirroring the complexities of actual life. To show you how it gets even more complex, the spheres of existence link to four realms of the cosmos. The first is the realm of pure mental rebirth, lacking any form. The second is the realm of pure form where the Gods reside. The third is the realm of desire containing the heavens, and spheres of the rebel Gods, animals, and humans. The last realm is that of the hungry ghosts and hell."

Piping in Fah suggested, "Maybe we are overwhelming them with information Gan. Perhaps it is time to move on with the tour."

"Yes, it is a great deal of information to absorb. What we will do at this point is see some of the other parts of Wat Pho. Most people just come for the Reclining Buddha, but the temple complex offers so much more."

Arriving at a courtyard and tower, he explained, "This is Phra Prang, one of four similar towers, each being lined with marbles." Hesitating as if trying to decide how much information to provide, he led us into the cloisters of the adjacent building, where numerous Buddha images line the walls. "You see how Wat Phro offers much more than the Reclining Buddha, but the giant takes most of the attention."

"Why show so many Buddha images in one place?" I felt the question had to be asked.

"I do not know for sure, but with Buddhism there is the notion of many forms, as with Hinduism. Siddhartha Gautama as the "Buddha" is only one Buddha, actually the twenty-fourth in this stage of the world. Then there are the Bodhisattvas, advanced spiritual beings related to Buddhas, who choose to help others achieve nirvana, this choice meaning that they stay in the cycles of rebirths."

Fah intervened at this point, "Gan is right that multiplicity of forms contributes to so many Buddha images in one location, but there is also a propaganda aspect: Many rulers advance their reputation by creating great temples, and Rama I, who got this temple going, is certainly such a leader. He rebuilt it on an earlier site, and some of his ashes are enshrined here. Rama III later added to it. Does that answer your question?"

"Yes, it does, and I get your point about propaganda; I've seen this same thing with different religions."

Looking at her watch, Fah explained, "We will briefly see a few other parts of Wat Phro, and then head to the Temple of the Golden Buddha. As you all have probably noted, the traffic and particularly around rush hours, can require the patience of Buddha, so we do not want to drive back to your hotel too late in the day."

For all the complexity of Buddhism, Wat Traimat housing the Golden Buddha, is strikingly simplistic and elegant. Demonstrating a European styling, the central staircase diverts to right and left, both sides taking visitors to the main temple entrance. Viewed from the bottom of the staircase, a triangular gold rimmed section, fronting a gold crowned tower, stands out. The numerous gold chofas, those bird-like images, along the edges of the tower, augment the power of the structure. Buddha, or Buddhas, would be pleased. Inside the temple itself, resides a gold Buddha sitting cross-legged, with his right hand on his right lower leg, and left hand facing up over his lap. Taller than a person, but much smaller than the Reclining Buddha while much larger than the Emerald Buddha, it conveys a strength from the near lifelike dimensions. A gold trimmed triangular background perfectly frames the statue.

Stating what I, and I suspect anyone who views the image, feels, Gan stated, "Perfection in a Buddha image, much like the temple building."

Seeing nods of affirmation, he continued, "The Golden Buddha has a very interesting story associated with it, somewhat like the Emerald Buddha. The image was covered in plaster and bits of glass, probably to hide it from Burmese invaders in 1767. The trick worked because the boring plaster statue was ignored, and it seems everyone connected to the deception passed away. Rama I brought statues to Bangkok to fill the temples he commissioned, and this was one of them. Rama III later transferred the plaster image to a temple in Chinatown. However, when this temple was closed, the statue was transferred here in 1935 sitting under a tin roof for twenty years. Then in 1954 a new structure was built to house it, and as the story goes, during the last attempt to lift the five-ton structure onto the pedestal, it fell to the ground. Some of the plaster came off revealing gold underneath. When the plaster was removed, they discovered a gold statue with nine parts fitting together perfectly, and a key at the base that could be used to disassemble the statue for easier transport! The body is 40% pure gold, the head 80%, and the hair 99%, with a value of maybe a quarter of a billion dollars or more! And just left in the open for years, and then under a tin roof."

As he ended a few of us vocalized, "Wow," simultaneously, and the rest were likely thinking it.

"The Golden Buddha was first housed in this new building in 2010, so quite recent. Speaking of recent we are going to show you a few of the sites of modern Bangkok, and try to get you back to your hotel well before dinner. How many of you are booked on the Wat Arun and river and lunch cruise for tomorrow?" All but two put up their hands. "Good, and that starts at eight o'clock as it is best to get to the temple earlier, and then we arrive for lunch at a very nice location."

For the rest of the tour that day I pretty much zoned out, feeling tired from the heat. In addition, modern Bangkok with its crowds and city smells seems very unappealing compared to the temples. Perhaps due to the way I'm feeling, it dawned on me that my exploration of major religions will soon be ending and I still do not have any revelation about life and death, and the afterlife. However, on the positive side, I feel confident that something will ultimately manifest.

We boarded the long and narrow motorized boat right at 8:00 AM, and docked at Wat Arun across the Chao Phraya River in under fifteen minutes. I, and everyone aboard, had already seen this amazing temple, from back on the hotel side, it rising up above the lower structures nearby. In the early morning and night, the latter from lights shining on it, Wat Arun really comes to life. Last night I sat in the open bar, mesmerized by the massive central tower, or prang, reaching to the heavens, and four smaller prangs at the corners. Now I actually get to experience it up close.

Gan interrupted my thoughts, "Unlike the other major temples in Bangkok, Wat Arun sits on the Thonburi side. It is on the site of an ancient temple, and at one point it housed the Emerald Buddha. Rama II restored the temple and extended the top to 70 meters. The prangs are encrusted with colored porcelain and seashells that were used for ballast in ships, making an artistic use of low value material. Those of you who have seen the temple at sunrise or at night know that it shines, and this is in part from the porcelain, and even shells." On the way past a corner prang he stopped enabling us to look at and touch the decorative pieces.

"Please examine the top of the tower." Noting upward gazes, he explained, "The central prang has a seven-prong trident that is known as the Trident of Shiva, the Hindu God responsible for the destruction phase of existence. In line with Buddhist beliefs, there are three levels to the temple, the base for all realms of existence, the middle where desires are realized, and the top six consisting of heavens with several realms of happiness."

From the second terrace, or for that matter, pretty much anywhere in the temple, the notion of levels is clear, based on the design in three progressively steeper sections. As I made my observations I couldn't help but notice more and more people occupying the stairs.

Aware of the crowds, Gan stated, "This is why we left earlier than most do. You do not want to be on these stairs at a really busy time." Gan and Fah quickly wrapped up the Wat Arun tour, and soon we were motoring along the Chao Phraya River. Initially, my gaze focused on Wat Arun, but then shifted to the river houses as we entered a residential section. It's amazing how people live in houses built over water on stilts, kids going to school in boats, and adults conducting their business the same way.

After about an hour we arrived at a more rural setting. Our guides gave us a tour of a small wat typical of most communities, containing a school for young children. Following this unique experience, we lunched in a large teak house along a canal, sampling a variety of traditional Thai foods. Gan and Fah entertained us with stories of life in Bangkok and the surrounding area, capping off the tour with this nice personal touch.

I struck gold with the tours so far, despite Gan in training, and now the authentic teak house on stilts with open windows, for the Chiang Mai stop of my Thailand and Buddhism odyssey. Following a relaxing half-day seeing the modern sites of this northern city, I felt ready for more wats. From what I read, being "watted out" from seeing too many similar temples is a common reaction for tourists who try and visit all the temples. To avoid this occurrence, I'm making it my last day of temple touring, the first stop being Wat Phra That Doi Suthep, located on a hill outside of Chang Mai. My guide, Hathai, a young and very polite woman, explained on the phone that this is the premier Buddhist temple in north Thailand.

The exertion expended walking up the hill certainly compensated for the limited exercise over the last few days. "This walk is different than the Buddhist temples in Bangkok." I was stating the obvious.

"Yes, the purpose is to convey a sense of power, that we are climbing to something special. We could have taken the tram, but this is a more authentic experience and you seem fit."

Special is an appropriate description based on the central gold covered stupa, and the gold umbrella like stands at the corners. Curious about them I asked, "What is the significance of these umbrellas?"

"They are an ancient symbol of kingship and are known as ceremonial umbrellas. Kings wished to align themselves with this temple as it is said to contain a piece of Buddha's shoulder bone. The legend says that a monk had a vision that a relic would be found in the Pang Cha area. He discovered a bone believing that it was from the shoulder of the Buddha. According to the legend it glowed, vanished, moved, and replicated itself."

"Must have been some powerful marijuana in the area." I couldn't resist the comment.

"Perhaps. When this monk took it to the local king it would not do any of those special things, and the king dismissed him. Another king, Nu Naone of Lan Na, heard of the relic and requested to see it. When the relic arrived, it broke into two pieces. The smaller piece was buried in a community temple, and the larger relic placed on the back of a white elephant released into the jungle. The elephant climbed Doi Suthep, stopped here, trumpeted three times, then died. The king interpreted this as an important omen or sign, and had the temple constructed at this location in about 1371. It was rebuilt in its present form in 1545."

Commenting more to myself, I expressed, "Amazing how one person can become so recognized."

"Siddhartha Gautama, the Buddha, gave the world such important knowledge that his recognition is certain."

"What knowledge stands out for you?"

"There is much but the Four Noble Truths are most important for me. He expressed that all existence is unsatisfactory and filled with suffering, dukkha. This is the first Noble Truth. The second is that dukkha arises from a craving or clinging, tamba, meaning a constant effort to find something permanent and stable in a transient world. The next Noble Truth is that dukkha can cease with nirvana, and the fourth is that nirvana can be achieved by following the Eightfold Path."

"The what?"

"It is a path to nirvana consisting of eight steps, although they do not have to be in sequence: Right understanding, right directed thought, right speech, right action, right livelihood, right effort, right mindfulness, and right concentration. The right understanding involves knowledge that all things are connected and dependent on each other, and only nirvana is independent. Related to the Eightfold Path is the Middle Path between self-indulgent pleasure and self-denial. Through these paths, nirvana, detachment, and freedom from births and rebirths, is achieved."

"That's a very good explanation."

"I'm a Buddhist and have studied it extensively."

"Wat," a slip of the tongue, "What makes a person a Buddhist?"

"There is no formal ceremony, unlike in some Western religions. It is really a matter of following the beliefs and practices. This is a major reason why it spread throughout the region including

Korea, Japan, China, Tibet, Thailand, and Indonesia. Of course, with the introduction of Islam to some areas it became more restricted."

"Are there different forms?"

"Yes, each region introduces some unique elements, although the core beliefs remain much the same. Here in Thailand we practice Theravada Buddhism, that adheres to the original texts."

"From what I've seen of other religions," suddenly I realized I have encountered a great deal in my travels, "branching out is normal, they never remain exactly the same."

"Buddha would agree, as nothing is permanent and stable, although we strive for it. What are you striving for?"

"I'm trying to see if there is a real meaning or purpose to existence, and what might occur beyond that. To achieve it I've been exploring major religions of the world."

"In many ways then you are searching like Siddhartha Gautama, and following the Eightfold Path. However, in at least this world everything is changing, and so you will not find a permanent answer from what you see here."

"Things always do seem to change."

"The only thing that is permanent is change."

During the rest of the day finishing the tour at Doi Suthep and the more minor Buddhist temples in the area, her words stuck with me, and kept replaying, such that I found it hard to concentrate on much of what else she expressed. My exploration of religion is ending, and there is still no actual answer, maybe because I'm looking for permanence in an impermanent world!

SECTION 3

THE DISCOVERY

INFORMATION BUT NO ANSWERS

My curiosity motivated me to explore the major religions of the world, and although saturated with information, I lack answers. Certainly, there are additional religions I might explore, even though the major ones have been covered, but somehow, I doubt further exploration of this kind will lead to any solid outcomes. Appreciating that relaxation can lead to insights, I travelled to Phuket, an island off Thailand renowned for good beaches, partying, and scuba diving. Booking on a so-called live-aboard dive boat, I'm looking forward to a week of scuba diving around the Similan Islands. Fortunately, I do not have to share the small cabin with a stranger, giving me a sense of privacy, and also room to move. I'm also fortunate that the sea is very calm, but since this is not always the case I have enough motion sickness medication to cover the trip. The other guests are from various parts of the world, all sharing a keen interest in diving.

    The sense of weightlessness always makes me feel as if I'm in flight; a very liberating experience. Flying over an underwater wall is like stepping off a cliff and defying gravity. Staring down into the abyss while making turns intensifies the experience of flight. Many people who do not scuba dive say that they would feel claustrophobic with all that water on them, but I experience freedom from the constraints of gravity. Science came to mind when I thought of gravity, and it leapt to the forefront of my thinking upon examining the corals. Even though most divers, largely uninformed about marine biology, see the reefs as fine, those with a background in science and interest in coral reef health, see something much different. Essentially, the reefs are dying!

    Much of the carbon dioxide we emit into the atmosphere from industrial activities is taken up by the oceans. While this carbon sink moderates global warming, it weakens anything relying on calcium carbonate, such as corals and shelled creatures, through a process known as acidification. In addition, warmer water is "bleaching" corals, a prelude to their death. Coral reefs are indeed being devastated, with scientists estimating that all will be gone well before the year 2100! It's a very sad reality, and even more depressing is how so many people, including scuba divers, deny the problem, thereby ensuring the demise of this unique ecosystem, and also largely unchecked carbon dioxide emissions. From what I've read, even transforming our major annual seed crops, such as wheat, corn, and rice, to perennials could massively ramp up the soil sink for carbon, removing much of what we have already placed in the atmosphere, potentially getting acidification and other global warming problems under control. Countries invest billions of dollars in weapons development, and no more than several million have been set aside for research into shifting our major crops from annuals to perennials.

Despite these disturbing thoughts regarding the health of coral reefs, I'm enjoying the trip and break from my quest. The motto with live-aboard diving is eat, sleep, and dive, which is pretty much how it's going on this trip, with a few hikes thrown in on some of the Similan Islands. On most days, there are three dives during the day and a night dive, the latter an experience not to be missed with the open expansiveness of the reef during the day, replaced with a focus on whatever your flashlight shines on, including reef sharks out hunting fish. Following the evening dive most of the guests go to bed exhausted, but having a robust energy level, I stay up enjoying a relaxing drink while watching the stars. Some nights a crew member and/or a fellow guest joins me, and this night it's the captain, Captain Ron, and no not as incompetent as the fictional movie captain, as well as a guest, Tony, an engineer from Seattle.

Drinks in hand, and bottoms resting on comfortable seats on the upper deck, partially open to the stars, I made the comment, "This must get pretty boring, Captain Ron, with all these stars most nights, and island scenery during the day."

"Makes me want to return to the city and see all those ugly buildings."

Chuckling at our humor, Tony, added, "Not to mention having to see the reefs every day instead of traffic."

"Yes, I tell people that my office is small but aquarium large. It's not for everyone living on the ocean, but I can't return to city life. I can visit, but have to come back to the ocean."

"What happens if and when the reefs die off, you know this global warming thing?" Even though I know it's negative, my thoughts about coral reefs needed to be expressed.

"I try and not think about it to stay positive, and fortunately most of the guests just want to identify fish they see. Many of those in the dive industry will not even acknowledge it's a problem, but I've seen the changes, read the articles, and call them like I see them, so I know it's true. One reason I moved here from the Caribbean where I captained a boat, is that most of the coral cover there is already gone, although few in the dive business will say so."

"That's sad, because if aware divers might advocate for change." Tony genuinely seemed disturbed. "I wonder why people avoid these realities?"

Familiar with this issue I piped in, "Based on my experience as a physician, and also just what I've observed generally, it's a defense to lighten stress. Instead of seeing the negative although often realistic, it's more comforting to see the positive. For example, people with terrible health habits, denying there's any reason for concern, and spinning it that things will be fine."

"I see that with most people, although there are the guests for whom everything is negative and a problem. You know, "Captain Ron, it's raining and shouldn't be this time of year." This type of comment all week long."

"The pessimists we all have to deal with. Good mental health is seeing the positive side, and the pessimists are vulnerable to depression and anxiety. I rarely see someone saying they're depressed who has a really positive outlook. Having an optimistic perspective and belief in something positive helps us cope."

"Even religious beliefs are a positive spin helping us cope with life when you think of it," added Tony. "I grew up in a Roman Catholic family, and it was all about God, and going to heaven if I did the right things. Being more scientific I had trouble accepting it even as a child, and then could not at all later when I really learned about science while studying engineering. However, I admire those who can spin it to see that God will take care of everything. How much easier life would be."

Zooming in on the religion slant initiated by Tony, I ventured, "I've been travelling to learn more about religious and spiritual beliefs, kind of a curiosity, although others have suggested it's more than that, and from what I've seen your comment is dead on: Religions do offer something far more positive than, "the end," that science seems to suggest." I suddenly realized that my immersion in religion has pushed science to the side. "Actually, in the process of learning about religion I've distanced myself from science."

"Maybe science is the pessimistic, like about global warming, and religion is the optimistic."

"Maybe, but when you study engineering and science do you feel negative and pessimistic?"

"No, I tend to feel enlightened if I'm looking into a concept, particularly when I'm encountering it for the first time."

"So, we can't say science is the pessimistic."

"Perhaps it's the realistic and religion more the fantasy or creative."

"I think so Tony, unless were talking about bias in research, which is a whole other topic. An incredible 80% of research results in medicine are false, and certainly not real, with many of these biased outcomes supporting products."

Remaining quite until this point, enjoying his beer and absorbing the conversation, Captain Ron ventured, "The real thing that's going on is science and religion never come together. You have science here," he extended his one arm away from his side while grasping an imaginary object in that hand, "and you have religion over here," extending the other arm and pretending to hold religion in that hand. "There's never any merging or bridging!"

"Yes, and by looking into religion I've been removing myself from science."

"And if you immerse yourself in science you distance yourself from religion, like I did when I entered engineering and took science to heart."

Smiling Captain Ron expressed, "Not a bad insight for a boat captain."

"Pretty amazing I'll say." I felt that Captain Ron captured the essence of the problem: Religion and science never merge!

"How can they ever merge though?"

"Ah, that is the ultimate question, Tony, and unfortunately I don't have the ultimate answer, at least yet."

"And the one who answers it gets the cigar. Speaking of cigars do either of you mind if I have one? Treat myself to one or two each cruise. I'll make sure the smoke drifts the other way." Realizing his social omission Captain Ron asked, "Do either of you want one?" When Tony and I failed to raise any objection, and declined his offer, Captain Ron lit up and slowly took a puff, the lights from the partial ceiling over the deck highlighting the rising cloud of smoke, it's presence etched into space for a brief moment before vanishing.

As we sat in silence for several minutes, I began thinking of the impermanence of things, such as the rising smoke. Here one moment and gone the next. The comment made by Hathai, my Chiang Mai guide, "…in at least this world everything is changing, and so you will not find a permanent answer from what you see here," it still sticking with me.

I decided to raise this with my new friends, "A wise person I met recently commented that I won't find a permanent answer in this world because everything is changing. I don't know if and how religion and science can ever merge, but if so the solution must have something to do with how transient things seem from a scientific perspective, and how religions provide a more permanent alternative."

"Maybe, it's just that science shows us an impermanent reality, and religion compensates for the negative implications by giving us a more hopeful option."

"Quite possible, Tony, but if there is a way to merge them it's got to solve the permanence/impermanence problem, at least regarding people and animals after they die. If we're just here like the cigar smoke one minute, or second, and then forever gone completely, how can religion and science ever merge?"

"Maybe they never will, but I agree that the answer needs to address that problem."

Stretching and yawning, Captain Ron, intervened, "Maybe you two need to relax your brains a bit more. That's what you're here for, and it's my job to help. If guests leave more stressed, I'm not doing my job" Pausing he added with a wide grin, "And I usually don't get much in the way of tips, more just complaints to the management. You might find that answers come easier after you take a break; I've often got that comment back from people after cruises, unless they're the type complaining about everything. I'm going to head off to bed now, since I have to get up early to move the boat to our next dive site."

Pausing for a second as if hesitating or trying to remember something, he added, "Regarding that permanence of life thing, there's a culture on the Indonesian island of Sulawesi, not too far from here by airplane, that's worth checking out. A few guests have travelled there and told me that these people don't view death as such a change, and often keep the deceased person with them. Sounds really weird, but it came to mind when you mentioned permanence of people and animals after they die."

I recalled hearing about them as well, the thought coming to mind around the time of "the horror," so his suggestion really peaked my interest. "Do you know what name they go by?"

"That's what I'm trying to remember, usually good with names, a person kind of has to be with so many guests. I know they're located in a Christian section of Sulawesi around the middle of the island. That's it, Torajans. The guests who went there said it was a very perspective changing experience."

"That's what I need at this point as I've got a lot of information and no answers."

"Would you mind if I come along, as this culture and your quest have really got my interest going? After this cruise, I planned on just winging it, seeing what strikes my fancy, and this does."

"Absolutely, Tony. Glad to have a friend along. We'll have to find out how to get there, but the journey shouldn't prove too difficult."

TORAJANS: IS DEATH THE END?

My comment to Tony suggesting that travel to see the Torajan people shouldn't prove too difficult was not exactly accurate. In fact, it was dead wrong. Flying to Bali, and spending a couple of days was easy and fun. However, flights to Makassar do not run every day, and the first one ended up being cancelled due to mechanical problems, and not one but two flat tires. When we finally made it to Makassar we learned that getting to Rantepao, the main Torajan town, involves a 200-mile bus journey. Way back with the "horror" that started my quest for answers, I travelled on a very modern state of the art bus. The one right in front of us could, I suppose, be described as state of the art thirty years ago. In the present very little actual paint remains, most windows lack glass providing natural air conditioning, and so much luggage is piled on the roof it appears to be sagging.

    Glancing at each other and shrugging our shoulders we climbed aboard, the interior proving to be in even worse condition, with most seats ripped and wrappers strewn about. At least the price is reasonable even in Indonesian rupiahs. I noticed several people carrying bibles in plain sight, and before long discovered why. After a brief stretch with only rolling hills, we entered mountains where the road corkscrews while clinging to cliff faces. Making matters more frightening, even if you've never experienced a bus accident like the "horror," we're seated on the valley side of the bus with me in the glassless window seat. I've heard that there are no atheists on the front lines, and considered asking one of the bible carriers if I could briefly borrow their book. However, most seem to be clutching the "good book" as if their life depends upon it.

    Silent for a long while Tony presented a point I failed to consider, "You realize that we have to come back this way?"

"I think my mind blocked that one out, but thanks for the reminder. Maybe there's a better option such as hiking through the jungle for weeks or months, and then swimming to the next island."

Laughing Tony expressed the obvious, "You don't like bus rides very much, do you?"

"No, my experience with buses hasn't always been so positive." I decided not to talk about the "horror," if for no other reason than reminding myself about bus crashes while on the bus ride from hell.

"A positive way of looking at this is that the bus and driver must have done it hundreds, if not thousands of times, and it's still working."

Considering his comment, I began to relax. The bus had obviously been in service for many years, and the driver didn't seem bothered at all, at least judging by his whistling to the music playing over the speakers. "You're right, even though it's new for us this route has likely been used for years." I tried not to look at some of the fellow passengers clutching their bibles.

Trying to distract myself I commented, "Interesting how Sulawesi is mostly Muslim, but some areas are Christian, such as the region of the Torajans."

"Apparently, it's due to the Dutch traders and missionaries that followed. They must maintain some of their original beliefs, though, as I don't recall any version of Christianity that maintains the dead. If anything, it's the opposite, making sure that the deceased are buried as soon as possible."

"Probably some unusual ancient culture, but I do recall that the Inca brought out the mummies of their deceased leaders for special occasions, and of course the ancient Egyptians tried to preserve their dead for the afterworld by mummifying them."

"So maybe the Torajans aren't all that unique in a historical context."

"In the present, though, they are distinct as I've never heard of any modern-day group keeping the deceased around."

"Neither have I, although many cultures have unique practices, even within a given religion."

"You can only imagine the Christian missionaries seeing dead people preserved and not buried. It must have shocked the hell out of them." We laughed at my dark humor.

"Well, that, and they might have reported additional members in their parish to get more funding."

"Just leaving out the part about them being dead."

"Details, only details."

"And that's coming from an engineer!"

"Then the supervisor comes and discovers half the parish members claimed."

"At least until introduced to the non-living members."

The humorous exchange lasted until we cleared the worst, or most scenic of the mountains, depending on your perspective, neither of us really noticing, being so focused on maintaining the lightness. Around yet another bend the road opened up into the large town, or small city, of Rantepao, the population reported at about 26,000. I wondered if this includes the living and dead, or just the former.

Exiting the bus, thankful to still be alive, we were greeted by a young twenty-something man, who in solid English said, "Welcome to Rantepao, and the Torajan people. My name is John. Might I help with accommodations and your luggage?"

First to speak Tony replied, "We do need a place to stay, but are not sure how it works here. Is there a motel?"

"Ah yes, there is, but you might not find it to be to your standards, and you will get less of the real Torajan experience."

"What do you suggest?"

"I have many contacts and can put you up in a good house sharing a room, but with separate beds."

It came to mind that in such a Christian, or for that matter Muslin, enclave, even a hint of homosexuality would not be looked at positively. Jumping in I stated, "Yes we do require two beds, but one room is okay, as long as it's clean. However, we don't wish to intrude into someone's home."

"The home of the family I have in mind is cleaner than the hotel, and they welcome guests for a small fee."

Looking at Tony, and noting him nodding in the affirmative, I asked, "How much is a "small fee" and in what currency?"

Satisfied with the answer in rupiahs, we shook hands with John. He effortlessly grabbed our luggage and led us to a modern four-wheel drive jeep. It surprised me seeing affluence in such a remote place, particularly after the bus experience. Most tropical cities and towns are not all that nice, from what I've seen, but this one appears neat and well kept, the roads also quite modern. Soon we pulled up to a large bungalow.

"I'll introduce you to the Rante family. There's the parents Elisabeth and Lassi, daughter Yohana, son Daniel, and grandfather Petrus."

Although dubious at first, John's arrangement and very reasonable costing appears to be spot on. Our room is larger than I thought it would be, brightly colored, with a large ceiling fan, and also its own bathroom. Based on our room and what I noted of the house passing through to the bedroom, it appears spotless.

The parents and children, seven-year old Yohana, and five-year old Daniel, also seem very friendly. We had yet to meet the grandfather. After freshening up, important with all the dust blown into the bus and sweat of fear, we joined the family in their spacious living room, where they had already set up tea and finger food.

First to speak, Lassi expressed, "We very much welcome you to our home, and to the Torajan people. We are aware that you have come to experience our culture, that while different than yours is natural to us."

Interjecting I mentioned, "I've been travelling to learn about world religions, and have encountered different cultures. My travel buddy is also familiar with various cultures."

"That is good because apparently, we are very different." Lassi let the words hang.

Curious about how fluent John, Lassi, and from what I could tell, the other Rante family members are in English, I had to say, "I didn't expect everyone to be so good with English."

Piping in Elisabeth explained, "Not everyone is, but many Torajans, such as ourselves, have traveled abroad for schooling and/or work, and return with new languages. My husband and I were educated in England, and worked there for a while. We have taught our children to speak English. There are some people here who have learned French, German, and other languages. When a guest arrives, Tony and the other greeters know what families to bring them to."

"That makes a lot of sense, and I'm very impressed as I assumed this would be an isolated society."

"There are many small communities that can take even days of travel to get to, and they usually do not leave, but those of us in Rantepao frequently do, although we almost always return. I believe that the money sent back from abroad, and certainly when converted to rupiahs, is more than what we make from crops grown and services provided, so living away from here actually helps keep us going."

Wondering how our time would be structured I raised the topic, "John didn't mention tours or other things we might do. Are you aware of how this usually works?"

Taking over for his wife, Lassi explained, "We will show you our culture, and have an event or two in mind. John will drive you to a smaller village, most likely, to see how they live. We do not plan out everything at the start, but go by the length of stay. How long will you be with us?"

Tony expressed, "We're flexible, maybe about a week." Looking at me he asked, "Is that about right?"

"Sounds reasonable."

"That good, because it will enable you to attend the main event we have in mind." Lassi smiled evidently pleased at the prospect.

"It sounds as if it's an important event." My curiosity triggered I want to find out what it involves.

"Yes, it's a celebration, a funeral."

"Who for?"

"Petrus, my father."

I now realize why Petrus wasn't there to greet us. Speaking for both of us I expressed, "We're sorry for your loss."

"Oh, do not be sorry as he is not lost, he is very much with us."

Hoping not to sound cruel I asked, "Don't you mean he was here?"

"No, he is still. This is a major way our culture differs from others; we do not believe that Petrus is gone, he remains with us and plays an important role."

"That is very different than our culture for sure, because when a person passes away they no longer have any role."

"Now that is very sad, and a real loss."

Considering Lassi's comment, I appreciate that we do have a very abrupt separation of life and death, with everything changing the instant a person dies. This of course jolts those who care into grieving, from zero to a hundred in seconds even. If a person still remains, in at least some form, then grieving must be all that much more gradual and gentle. "Yes, I think you're right, and we often say, "Here today, gone tomorrow," to express that change. It is a radical shift and change in status. A person could be a leader and respected, and then no more."

"Petrus is a community leader and many will come to celebrate at his funeral. It is a major event in our community, and will occur five days from now."

Tony asked, "Where's your father now?"

"He is in the room next to yours!"

"Next to ours?" Even having heard about how the dead are kept in the family for a time, I still found myself reacting with shock. I assumed that the person would be in a shed outside or some other enclosure.

"Yes, and it is now time to bring him tea and a snack, although his appetite is less than usual." Picking up a prepared tray with a tea kettle, cup, and plate of food, Lassi walked towards the bedroom next to ours, pausing at the door and looking back, "Grandfather takes his tea at this time, so please come."

Feeling a strange mixture of revulsion and curiosity, I stood and made for the door, noting Tony following. Inside the room lay Petrus propped up on the bed with a couple of pillows, a baseball cap firmly on his head. His clothes and degree of preservation make it appear that he will just get up and walk.

Noting me looking at the baseball cap, Lassi explained, "It's his favorite."

The baseball cap somehow both countered and added to the ridiculousness of the situation, at least from the perspective of our culture, and I started feeling a compulsion to laugh. I checked my humor before creating an embarrassing situation. Unfortunately, my comment probably created more embarrassment than laughter would have, "He almost looks alive."

Silence followed before Elisabeth responded, "But he is still alive in that his being is here."

Feeling disoriented and confused, I tried to dig myself out of the social transgression, "I meant his physical appearance makes him look real."

Sensing that I had succeeded in putting both feet in my mouth, Tony intervened, "My friend is expressing what we are feeling—shock and confusion—because this is so different than what we're used to. I also think he's referring to the preservation technique for Petrus's physical form." Seeing everyone relax, other than the apparently always relaxed kids who each held one of Petrus's arms pretending to tickle him, Tony asked, "What's your technique?"

Although not identifying with being gay, I wanted to kiss Tony for his diplomatic intervention.

"Ah, really quite simple and effective: We apply formalin, which is formaldehyde plus water, so the body mummifies over time, and does not decay."

"Amazing!" I thought by limiting myself to a one-word response I could avoid disturbing my hosts, although they seemed to not care about my comments, taking it in stride.

Clearing Yohana and Daniel away, Lassi stated, "Here's your tea father." Placing the tray on a stand by his father he explained, "We refer to the dead as macula, meaning a sick person, and one who is still present. The soul remains connected to us even after the funeral, so we do not view a person as being departed. The funeral is a celebration, and can last a week even. Some families keep the person with them for weeks, months, and even years until all the person's relatives and friends can come, no matter how far. You are fortunate, as all those who know Petrus are now here, a couple of months after he started experiencing macula, and we are ready for the great event."

Feeling my head clear from the shock, I found there to be a contradiction. "I'm not sure I understand why a funeral is so important if the person is still present."

"Because we wish to honor him or her, and make them feel at peace." Lassi's explanation made perfect sense.

Adding to her husband's explanation, Elisabeth expressed, "There is also the matter of status in the community for the family, with bigger funerals reflecting a higher standing. The money we are putting into Petrus's funeral might mean no money for our kids' weddings, or higher education, but to us death trumps life."

Although this seems very odd, I refrained from commenting, having only two feet to put in my mouth.

Gradually we both acclimatized to the notion of a dead person, or sick to our Torajan hosts, being in the bedroom next to us. It is amazing what you can adjust to, and I even started saying, "Morning Petrus," as I passed his room on my way to breakfast. Tony caught on to my greeting and also expressed it. Over the next few days our hosts took us to meet relatives and friends, a few also living with the deceased, to our way of thinking. Today we embarked on a different experience, John driving us to a small village along a very rutted dirt road, or more track, that required engaging the four-wheel drive all the way.

On a somewhat smoother section requiring less focus he asked, "How's it going with your new family?"

I responded first, "Very well, and thanks for setting us up with them. They're very nice, and as you mentioned when we arrived, this is a real Torajan experience."

Tony piped in, "It took a bit of getting used to having deceased Petrus in the next room. Oddly, we don't even smell anything."

"At first there can be a smell, but we live in a very hot climate so windows are always open and fans on. Do you see Petrus from the Torajan perspective?"

Hesitating briefly considering what John meant, I replied, "Death is not seen as an abrupt change, but more of a gradual process."

"That is so, and we do not view a person as gone, as they continue to exist."

"But in what form?" My interest soaring as I sensed a potential answer to my quest.

"That we are not sure of, but they do continue on."

I felt my hope for an answer fading fast. "Do you mean that their spirit or soul persists?"

"Yes, but also that they are still close to us and not really "dead." This is much different than being in some distant heaven or hell, as the Christian religion says."

"But most of your people are Christian."

"We take the parts that work for us, while keeping our own cultural beliefs."

I thought of other religions I encountered such as the Objibwe and Anishanaabe more generally, where spirits of people, animals, and objects persist, noting the similarity, although they do not retain the bodies of their deceased and do see them as truly dead. "How did Torajan beliefs start?"

"According to archeologists our beliefs and practices began around 900 years after Christ, but none of us really know for sure. In a few minutes we will arrive at a typical Torajan village, and you will see that recording events is not a priority."

After a few more spine jarring rebounds from tire-swallowing ruts, we arrived at our destination. As with so many rural towns kids ran about carefree, with adults less visible.

"Towns such as this one do not have electricity and might have a few vehicles at most; they have to transport gas from Rantepao. Often there is no schooling beyond religious instruction, and almost everyone works tending small plots or collecting fruit from the forest. This village is probably the most advanced and with the best road."

Interrupting him I exclaimed, "It's hard to imagine a worse road."

"Oh, let me assure you that we have much worse. This one has tire size ruts; some have jeep size ruts!"

"That's amazing."

"As is what you will witness today. Other than this being the closest town, and yes with the best road, today a family I know is having what we often refer to as a second funeral." He did not elaborate at this point.

From the crowd outside one small house, I assumed, and correctly so as it turned out, that this is the funeral family. After a very quick introduction, given how busy everyone seemed to be, we joined a procession along a jungle path to a nice spot overlooking a valley. It clearly served as a cemetery judging by several rough stone crypts. The father and his two teenage children pulled back a rock covering one of the crypts, before disappearing inside.

A few moments later with the father supporting her right arm, and the teenagers her left, emerged the mother. The sight of the former woman, now with black eyes, mottled and lesioned skin, stringy hair, and withered body covered by tattered decaying clothes shocked both of us, when we thought we were beyond it all at this point. The family were talking to her in their native language, but John interpreted.

"They are saying that they love her and it is time for her to get some sun and fresh air. Also, that new clothes are needed."

At this point the father and teenagers lay the mother on the ground, and began replacing her clothes with new garments. They also brushed the remaining hairs, and lay cigarettes and snacks beside her. I couldn't help thinking that the cigarettes were likely the reason for macula. After some further words that John indicated were more words of affection mixed with prayers, the mother was returned to the crypt along with her cigarettes and snacks. The rock panel replaced, our procession returned to the village where we enjoyed a very filling lunch served outdoors.

I thought we'd seen everything unusual that the Torajan culture has to offer, but John explained that something even more unique is to be experienced, the funeral for Petrus. Upon returning to Rantepao, he also explained that our host family will be so busy on the first of the funeral days that he will fetch us next morning.

Leaving his jeep at the Rante's house, John led us a few blocks to a community park where unique buildings surround a dirt square: Each building has a roof that extends out and upwards to a point, one having a thatched roof made of palm fronds, and the others wood or some type of paneling. Only one of the buildings has a closed front, people lining the inner open section of the other buildings. In addition, concession stands, clearly modern in design with printed advertisements for beverages, sit between the more traditional buildings.

In contrast to any funeral I've attended, the general atmosphere seems downright festive. I feel like I'm at a concert or at least a cultural show, and the music blasting over speakers supports this perspective. Shortly, a man's voice replaced the music, speaking the same language we encountered yesterday at the rural town.

Glancing at John for interpretation, he explained, "The announcer is asking that the person who has the black jeep parked out front please move it as it's blocking the buffalo."

Laughing I responded, "The what?"

"Buffalo, they're part of the funeral."

I refrained from asking what part, sure I would soon find out. Tony also held himself back from asking.

I surmised that the jeep had been moved based on ten buffalo entering the central square, followed by the Rante family, along with extended relatives. Not seeing the key player in the festivities, I asked, "Where's Petrus?"

"Oh, he's over there sitting in that large chair." John pointed to the building across from us, the seat mostly obscured by onlookers. As the Rante family stepped onto the platform the crowd cleared to let them stand beside Petrus. Taking turns at the microphone, Lassi and Elisabeth spoke.

"They're praising Petrus for all his contributions to their family and community, and also welcoming relatives not seen for a time. You can miss a wedding, and no one really minds, but to miss a funeral is another story; a sign of disrespect."

Tony expressed, "It's more the opposite in our culture, with people often avoiding funerals, as they're too depressing."

"Torajan funerals are a party, and a time of celebration, not at all depressing."

"Reminds me of an Irish wake, where the person's life is celebrated."

With the speeches by Lassi and Elisabeth, and also a few community leaders, finished, a young strong looking man walked out amongst the buffalo. Approaching the closest, he raised a long and lethal looking knife to the buffalo's throat, slitting it.

We sat in stunned disbelief as the first buffalo bled from its neck, the flow of red clearly visible. After a couple of minutes and almost in slow motion, it sank to the ground rolling onto its side, legs kicking spasmodically before ceasing to move. The young man repeated this procedure with the remaining buffalo to cheers from the crowd.

The sight of ten previously healthy buffalo now lying dead on the ground, dirt mixed with blood, almost made me want to vomit, and I likely would have if not for my shocked state of mind; I felt completely numb. Despite my mental state, John's words broke through.

"I know this is shocking to you, but it is our way, the sacrifice of buffalo and other animals, such as pigs, part of the ceremony. The family is honoring Petrus and giving to the community—We are going to be eating a lot of buffalo for a while. Each buffalo is worth about fifteen hundred US dollars, so the family has sacrificed greatly to provide this celebration."

Shaking away the numbness, I replied, "I can see why the family mentioned it could take away from their children's weddings or education."

"To not do this would result in a diminished status for the children, worse than no marriage or education." After a pause he added, "And Petrus is undoubtedly very pleased."

Recovering from the initial shock, despite still staring at the dead buffalo, it came to mind that almost all religions I've encountered have a sacrifice built into them, that at least initially involved animals and/or people. In Christianity, Jesus made the sacrifice, but to the Christian Torajans, animals still have to be part of it.

"I know it's part of the culture, but it seems awfully cruel." Tony expressed my exact thoughts.

"Maybe, but think of the meat you eat back home with animals kept in cramped conditions, pumped full of hormones and antibiotics, then slaughtered on an assembly line. Is this really cruel in comparison? These animals have been well fed, and free to roam in good enclosures, and then they have this one really bad day, for them, perhaps aware that they are part of a great celebration."

Seemingly less disturbed, Tony ventured, "When you frame it like that, I can see how it's not so bad, just shocking to us."

"Yes, because you hide death, whereas to us it is not so different than life. We are not ashamed of it, seeing it as a personal failing or poor medicine, it is just another stitch in the fabric of life."

I know that John's explanation contains a key to my quest, but it alludes me as to what. Late that evening sitting outside the Rante's house with Tony I decided to raise my thoughts.

"That explanation John gave about death being just another stitch in the fabric of life, I know it holds some crucial meaning, but I can't put it together."

"Yes, it does seem profound. What comes to mind when you think about it?"

"As you might recall me mentioning back on the dive boat, during my tour in Chiang Mai the guide said that I will not find a permanent answer in this world because everything is changing. The Torajans do not seem to see the world in the same way, more that there is permanence and a person continues even when dead, or as they would say, sick."

"They do believe that things continue on, although they don't seem entirely clear as to the form."

"It's almost more than that, though, because other religions believe that we continue on, such as to some heaven or hell, but they see it as a part of life, just different, like sections of a garment stitched together. Somehow, it's present around us."

"That is very different and a unique way of looking at it."

"I suspect it holds a key, maybe even the key to my quest."

"Even though I'm not bad at this conceptual spiritual stuff for an engineer, you seem way ahead of me on it. Now if you want me to explain principles of electrical engineering I can help, but with this, I think you're on your own."

"Well, we'll be together for the next few days at least, as we make our way back to Bali, but then I think you're right. However, let's make sure we keep in contact, and who knows, I might come up with something."

"Sounds good to me, and always happy to help out."

"I appreciate that, Tony. You've helped already."

"Glad to be of assistance. By the way, do you think that we should purchase a couple of bibles for the return bus ride?"

"No, we'll continue on here in some form even if we go over a cliff."

"Now that's the Torajan spirit."

A HEAVENLY PARADISE

Hawaii was described as a paradise by Paul Theroux in his book, The Happy Isles of Oceania: Paddling the Pacific, and it was his last destination after kayaking many islands in that vast Ocean. This is also going to be the last exotic destination on my journey of discovery, and I'm curious to see how much of a paradise it is. My plan involves a week or so on the "Big Island" of Hawaii, followed by few days in Honolulu at Waikiki Beach. Given the late arrival at Oahu I opted to stay at an airport hotel, and depart for the "Big Island" the next day.

Baggage arriving intact, I made my way from the luggage carousel to the hotel courtesy phone. A short shuttle ride is required, so technically it isn't really at the airport. Five attempts later, after just getting a recorded message about how great the hotel is, I gave up on calling. If one strategy fails, try another, so I exited to where taxis and buses arrive. Several minutes later I found an airport employee who directed me to the right place to wait.

Relief when the shuttle bus arrived turned to intense frustration at the hotel, upon finding a massive lineup and only two slow check-in staff. Making matters worse, most of those in line were Japanese and few spoke English, nor did the hotel staff speak Japanese, or at least very well. Tiredness and frustration prompted me to speak up loudly and assertively to a male hotel employee, wearing a manager label on his suit jacket, who just stood at the back watching. I requested that he open another check-in desk even if he had to work. His look of annoyance was more than compensated for by the favorable looks and "Ya," "It's about time," and the like from the English-speaking guests. So far, Hawaii is not a paradise.

The basic but comfortable room I eventually acquired compensated somewhat for the hassles, and I did sleep well.

Waking refreshed I feel optimistic that today will work out better than my arrival. For domestic flights the hotel staff suggested that two hours is more than fine. Deciding to play it safe, I left the hotel three hours earlier, and am thankful I did, because "enhanced security" took over an hour before I even made it to the Hawaiian Airlines counter. With only two hours I might have missed the flight. The hassles hopefully out of the way, I have just under an hour to relax in the dated domestic terminal.

While virtually every other airline in the world is going with less carry-on luggage, Hawaiian Airlines lets virtually anything on, such as the large cooler the middle-age couple from the deep south of the United States, judging by their accent, tried to shove into the overhead bin, and eventually rammed under my seat positioned just ahead of them. The promotions for Hawaii never show what I've been going through since arrival, but with the flight underway and clear skies, I settled back and looked at the islands below trying to work out which ones they are.

Relative to the Oahu arrival yesterday, things are starting well on the "Big Island." The location of the shuttle bus to the car rental agency I booked online with, is clearly marked, and within a half-hour I'm seated in a jeep ready to roll. I want to make sure I have four-wheel capacity just in case the need arises.

The journey south to the Kailua-Kona area is what I imagine driving along a lunar landscape to be like, with all the dark volcanic rock on both sides. Mostly scrub brush grows in this area, and the only trees are closer to the ocean.

Prior to arriving, I decided to split my stay between the Kailua-Kona area and the Kohala coast north of the airport, where the best beaches are reported to be. My first destination, the Courtyard King Kamehameha Kona Beach Hotel, is located in the main tourist section of Kailua-Kona. I can't help but to compare the lobby and reception here to the airport hotel, the spaciousness of the King Kamehameha and friendly fast service such a welcome relief. I strolled through a long room with windows on one side before arriving at the elevators. The very cool air and eye soothing colors of the carpet, such a contrast to the heat and brightness of the sun outside. I marveled at a large game fish mounted on a pedestal, wondering if any more fish of that size actually exist around Hawaii given all the overfishing plaguing the world. My fourth-floor room looks out over a flat roof to the small beach and shrine to the king himself, and no not Elvis Presley. Yes, this is a good place to be, and maybe paradise?

Paradise came but not in the form I expected. During my time in India and Southeast Asia, I remained in contact with Aminta, her expressing a desire to meet me in Hawaii. However, she doubted she could get away, and it's a long journey. Based on our last communication it seemed that she would not be coming, although she did take note of the hotels and dates I booked, so I focused myself on another solo journey. Then came the call later in the afternoon my first day on the "Big Island." Instead of back in Greece she's in the lobby of the King Kamehameha! What a surprise, and not the hour wait to go through "enhanced security" type.

Passion and not words consumed us for the next couple of hours, although time seemed to not matter anymore, the experience making me feel like I'm in a heavenly paradise. It's incredible how relaxed a person can feel after romance, and surprises me how tense I must have been, perhaps due to travel hassles in "paradise," and/or not finding any clear answers yet to the big questions. Maybe there are no answers, and only questions? I decided to focus on sightseeing, including Aminta's curvaceous body, and not try so hard for a solution.

As day faded to night, we took a stroll along the Kailua-Kona waterfront. Facing west, the view of the setting sun is mesmerizing, the large radiant orb contacting the horizon, and then slowly merging with it before being consumed. Having satisfied our visual sense, we focused on satiating our gustatory sense, the search for a good restaurant being very easy with the abundance. The availability of a table right by the seashore settled the deal, and we settled in for dinner.

After ordering two Kailua Sunset drinks I expressed what I'm feeling, "I'm still shocked that you're here, and we're actually facing each other, and not just face timing on a device."

"I thought you'd be surprised. So much better than if I said I'm coming and then couldn't make it."

"True, very true. When your experience exceeds expectations, you feel good, but bad when experience falls short of expectations."

"Speaking of expectations, what do you think we should do while we're here?"

Smiling to make sure she knows I'm joking, since humor often is hard to communicate between different cultures, I expressed, "Well now that we've got that sex thing out of the way, maybe we should plan some hikes."

Turning to reveal her shapely legs she exclaimed, "You want to get these out of the way?"

Going with her humor I replied, "Maybe I should rephrase my statement."

"Good idea, or you won't be seeing these and various other appealing aspects of your girlfriend."

"Between love making with such a beautiful and amazing Goddess, I think we should do some hikes."

"Much better!"

"Also on hikes I can see those legs of yours if you're in the lead."

"Well, let us pick a long one then so you get your fill."

"I read a book about hikes here during the flight from Southeast Asia, and it mentioned that the best is probably one at Volcanoes National Park, the Kilauea Iki Crater Trail, that actually goes down to the floor of the volcano."

"That sounds really interesting, but is it not dangerous?"

"Oh no, the volcano erupted in that location back in 1959, and now it's solid volcanic rock. This island is one of the few places in the world that even with rising sea levels from global warming, is actually adding land. There's a massive lava vent positioned right below Volcanoes National Park, a good place for a park with that name, that never moves. Instead as the tectonic plate above it passes over, lava pores out forming the Hawaiian Islands. Kauai to the north is the oldest, although the remote northern islands that are currently atolls are actually older, having passed by the hotspot many eons ago. Now it is the "Big Islands" turn."

"Wow, that's really exciting. I didn't know you're a geologist too."

"Just curious and take an interest in things."

"We share that and will share that hike tomorrow."

During the meal we considered other possible excursions, and decided upon a helicopter ride around the island, a drive tour down the east coast, and hike to a valley on the northeast coast, the latter two options when we shift to the Kohala coast in a few days. The meal lived up to expectations, and so did the remainder of the night including a walk and more love-making. Yes, I think that Hawaii is a heavenly paradise.

Refreshed from a deep peaceful sleep, I woke just after sunrise, looking forward to what the day will bring. Following a quick buffet breakfast on the outdoor terrace of the hotel restaurant, we assembled what we thought will be needed for the day, and headed out.

If Volcanoes National Park at all matches the scenery along the west coast, we will indeed be in for a great day. The first half or so of the route south taking us up and down and around hills, with the ocean to the right side, often far down steep inclines. This is not the road to drive tired or impaired along, for sure. Then nearing the southern end of the "Big Island," that is the southernmost point in the United States, we turned inland, passing through forested areas. We both noticed the temperature dropping and also fog, that I read is called, vog, for volcanic fog. Most shocking is how suddenly, even though it's probably more gradual, the climate shifts from tropical to temperate. The vog really drove this point, and with it the much cooler temperature, home.

After paying for a park pass we entered the information center, also serving as a gift shop, and purchased a couple of long sleeve shirts. Although trying to be diligent, we forgot to consider that it could be cooler at the park. With directions and a trail map in hand, we drove the short distance to the Thurston Lava Tube.

Having researched the trails, I stated, "This is a good starting point for the Kilauea Iki Crater trail, and apparently really interesting to see in itself."

"You be the guide then."

"But you have to lead sometimes so I can see those legs of yours."

Entering the Thurston Lava Tube, she replied, "You won't see much with the light in here."

Lights along the tunnel made it suitably lite, but not for seeing things in detail. Fulfilling my new role as tour guide, I explained, "I read that Hawaiian volcanoes are distinct because the lava always oozes and flows, instead of like those volcanoes that just explode. Lava tubes are where the lava flowed and the top of the flow cooled and hardened, creating a tunnel when the rest of the lava drained."

"Very good Mr. Tour Guide, I'll have to give you a tip later, back in our room, and see if something else flows."

"If that was the standard tip, I think tour guide would be a saturated job."

"Carry-on and tell me more."

Going with the flow and exiting the lava tube, I responded, "All these trees and ferns are due to the rich volcanic soil. The region we passed driving here is where Kona coffee, some of the best in the world is grown, due to the rich soil."

"It's amazing how things are so different from one part of the island to the other, with this area so lush, and by the airport so arid."

"From what I've read that's the most unique feature of the island."

Finishing the short trail and back on the road, Aminta asked, "So where to now?"

"Right across the road and a very short walk we start the trail to Iki Crater."

"You really are a good tour guide."

"I try and please."

With the sun breaking through it felt hot again, so we removed and packed our long sleeve shirts, just wearing the short-sleeve shirts underneath. A few minutes into the trail the vegetation on the left opened up, exposing the crater way below. Noticing small objects moving I commented, "Those people down there look like ants."

"That's where we're heading?"

"Yes, down one side, across the crater floor, and up to where we parked."

Wanting to capture the moment, Aminta took out her camera and snapped several pictures, something she repeated along the way, getting me in some, and I taking the camera and getting her in a few. Seeing another photographer, I asked if he could take a photo of us both, with the vegetation around and above us nicely framing the image.

As the trail descended the insects became human in dimension and form, and shortly we emerged on the floor of the crater. "There are people up there looking down at us now, and thinking we're like ants."

"It's all in the perspective," replied Aminta.

Taking the opportunity to discuss my odyssey, I stated, "That's one thing I have learned from my travels to uncover the big picture. There are just so many perspectives regarding religion and the nature of the cosmos."

"And you wish to get the big picture now that you're on the "Big Island," is that so?"

"Yes, but I'd be happy to get it sitting on a toilet in a gas station back home."

Laughing she replied, "Pease don't say that the answer is, "Everything is crap," as you did not need to travel so much to discover that."

"No, I don't think it's crap. I do believe there's a pattern to it all, but it's so elusive and complex."

"Let's see if we can break it down."

Walking across the flat volcanic rock of the crater floor, noting vog rising from vents, and small grass like plants striving to put life into the crater, I thought how I might start expressing the information I've acquired. The plants gave me an idea, "It's almost like with these plants striving to grow, in that people generate religious beliefs."

"Very true, but why do you think we do it?"

"Unlike plants and most, or maybe all, animals, we are the only ones with the ability to see our deaths, and know what it means. That's such a horrible reality we're all motivated to create a more pleasing alternative, and that alternative is religious beliefs."

"But what about religions, such as that of my ancestors, that are light on after death options?"

"As you so well explained it that first day we met, cult religious beliefs arose, often specific to particular regions, to provide the hopeful option. So even if the main belief system is light on after death options, more specialized parts develop it."

"Good point, but what you're suggesting means that maybe the toilet view is right—It's all crap of sorts to make us feel better. Consider how people defend their beliefs and insist they're right when there is no proof, no science behind them. This type of reaction and the strength, think of that terrorist you encountered, suggests they're protecting a notion they need, the belief in something beyond this world."

I thought of Captain Ron and his perspective that science and religion never mesh. "And if it's all about a defensive belief system then science cannot play a role, because the truth is not valued!"

"Like others, I have spiritual beliefs, but I'm afraid that you might have discovered the answer: It's all a creation to defend against the notion of us passing. Of course, add in motivation for social cohesion, as with the Ten Commandments."

"Our psychological defenses are very strong, and it would be a mistake to underestimate the influence of them. Believing in an afterlife is very reassuring, unless it's hell or a bad rebirth in Hinduism or Buddhism."

"True, and the options proposed for an afterlife are all over the map."

"You're right: The ancient Egyptians passage into the afterlife if your life is judged to be good; the monotheistic Big 3 heaven and hell; the ancient Greeks various often secretive options under cult religions; the ancient Romans, Fields of Elysium for warriors, the Plain of Asphodel for good people, and a tortuous visit to Tartarus for those who have been bad; Mayan people the underworld, but possibility of paradise; the Inca upper and lower realms, with a good person entering the former and participating in the lives of those still living, whereas those who are bad enter the underworld condemned to a cold existence; Anishanaabe, and many other First Nations, spirits continuing on around us; cycles of rebirth with Hinduism and Buddhism, the former with a permanent soul and the latter without one."

"Even with such a wide range of options, there is not a shred of evidence supporting any of them!"

"In a very real sense it's false hope, and aligns with our tendency to not only defend against negative realities, such as death, but to separate body and soul. I recall reading that we naturally separate the physical and mental, like body and mind, when they are all based in biology, as with the mind part of the brain, and hence cannot be separated."

"Then beyond the complete lack of evidence for an actual afterlife, there is a clear reason why the notion of an actual soul continuing on is incorrect. To believe in an afterlife a person has to reject science and remain in the dark."

"That's interesting, Aminta, because by rejecting science, those who believe in something more than this life might be resigning themselves to not discovering that there really is something greater, ironically. They adhere to completely outdated notions, such as Adam and Eve, blocking any revelations that might come from science."

"But science rejects religion, and even if scientists believe in religion they, how do you say it, put them in separate bins?"

"Compartmentalize them, so they do not seek an answer either."

The conversation was so absorbing that neither of us realized that the sun had turned to cloud and rain was starting to fall. Only halfway across the crater floor, and completely exposed, we stopped both the conversation and walking to store Aminta's camera, and put on the plastic rain slicks we thoughtfully packed.

Resuming the walk, now protected from the rain, I resumed the conversation. "I do believe that the ultimate answer must somehow synthesize science and spiritual beliefs. Where those with religious beliefs have it right is by actually believing in something. Hard core scientists believe in nothing other than science as a methodology, an approach to solving problems through experiments, and also theories that provide a best of fit with the experimental data, but many don't even bother with the latter. It's devoid of any meaning, and highly limited, particularly if theory is rejected."

"What aspects of religious belief relate to science? Perhaps if we can identify them it might help merge the two."

"Very good point. One might be that somehow an essence of us persists. That is definitely a common theme. The Anishinaabe believe, as do many First Nations peoples, that everything carries on. That rock over there and plant beside it, persist in some form."

"Maybe there is something to the notion of persistence."

"The Torajans take this notion to the extreme, actually believing that a deceased person is still present here, just ill!"

"I find your stories of them really interesting, but also creepy."

"The creepy part I also thought at first, but staying with them for a while and having grandfather Petrus in the next bedroom, dead and all, my views shifted. We're so embedded in the notion of death being final, hard stop, but they see it much differently."

"Persistence of some form or essence is almost certainly a contribution of religion to the larger picture, and also merging science and religion, but the big question is, what form does that take?"

Reaching the end of the crater floor we started up a path, that like the one on the way down, resembles a tunnel with vegetation growing over it. The rain seemed to be ending and the sun broke through from time to time. Exertion of the uphill hike suspended mentally challenging conversation, and certainly any producing a viable answer to Aminta's question.

Hunger informed us that it's lunch time. We located a quaint and surprising good restaurant, Ohelo Café, in Volcano Village. Although we could sit outside, the vog and coolness of the air motivated us to take a table indoors. The wood décor and old fashioned tables triggering a fantasy of coming to the park in the 1950's, and seeing the crater that we just crossed erupting. The waitress interrupted my fantasy, but given my hungry state I did not mind in the least. We decided to share a pizza.

The pizza and drinks refreshed us helping restart the conversation. "So now that we've done the best hike, what does my tour guide suggest we do next?" Smiling she added, "Consider that your tip tonight might depend on the quality of the afternoon hike."

"The pressure's on now! I think that we we'll more drive than hike, going along Chain of Craters Road, taking us right to the ocean."

"Sounds good."

"From what I read it is."

"So far, your guiding has been solid, so I trust your decision. Besides, we're having such a good time together."

"Yes, we are, very good. That hike was so much more interesting with you than it would have been on my own, and the conversation has been very helpful."

"But we, or maybe I should have said, "you," are not much closer to an answer."

"The term "We" is okay, I like the sound and feel of it, and you're helping narrow things down, so there is progress."

"Do you have any further insights?"

"Another common feature of religions that comes to mind is how they so well reflect or capture human nature."

"Such as?"

"There's the hierarchy aspect that is very common, as in rankings within the given religion, or amongst Gods and Goddesses if there is polytheism. Of course, a God or Goddess has a higher ranking than a person. It mirrors our proclivity to form hierarchies, such as with me the boss here."

Winking she replied, "You're my tour guide, and that makes me the boss."

"Okay, boss. There's also the notion of good and bad behavior relative to the social group, and rewards like heaven or a good reincarnation for positive behavior, and punishment with various forms of hell or a bad reincarnation for antisocial behavior. Religions usually specify what constitutes good and bad behavior."

"A very clear social cohesion role, and this also gives a group a clear identity."

"You're right. However, these other aspects do not really help us with what might merge science and religion, as they're social functions."

"I see and feel what you're going through trying to sort all this out. What we need to do is put it aside for a while, and see if anything we encounter triggers more thoughts."

"Good idea, boss. If you're finished your meal let's take a drive."

We shortly discovered that Chain of Craters Road is apply named, based on all the craters from prior eruptions, most a minute or so walk from the car. As the road descended the vog cleared and past lava flows stood out. The switchback design of the road emphasizing the nature of the lava flows, as we continually observed upwards to the craters and downwards to the sea.

At sea level, we walked to the edge of the island, the drop to the ocean preventing any chance of standing on the shore. Holei Sea Arch, formed from waves carving an arch out of a volcanic rock extrusion over countless years, seemingly providing a doorway to the ocean. Looking inland I tried to imagine a flow from the top right to the sea, with the boiling lava cooling as it merges with the ocean. What a sight that would be! We took a walk further down the road extending along the coast, drawn to a cluster of palm trees on an escarpment by the water. Standing out amongst the trees are very unique lava patterns, one shaped like a turtle, with colorful flowers framing the images.

On the drive back up, we stopped at an ancient Hawaiian site, where petroglyphs were carved, giving these long-departed peoples, a slice of immortality.

At one petroglyph Aminta commented, "Look at the woman and small child. You can almost picture them lying side-by-side together."

Having just read one of the information signs, I commented, "Apparently, these people placed the umbilical cord in the holes you see in this and the other images. They believed it brought good luck to the baby."

My own words triggered a thought, "That's another common aspect of religions—They seem to require a sacrifice of some form." The gruesome image of the buffalo slaughter at Petrus's funeral forced itself into consciousness, but I pushed it out. "It's like life for life in a sense."

"That is consistent with what I've learned about religions in my own studies. Think of all the sacrifices the ancient Greeks made to their major and cult Gods and Goddesses, and Jesus making the sacrifice for all Christians."

"Very generous of him."

"If this sacrifice aspect to religion was not so prominent, then Jesus would have a different fate, maybe living on."

"Now that's an interesting perspective."

"Let's see what else we can identify in these images."

Scrutinizing several, I note that most contain representations of people with arms and legs extended, suggesting to me sexual or reproductive meanings. Noting what looked like a bicycle, I commented, "Oh, and they got around on bicycles, see here."

Laughing she replied, "Your tour guiding is slipping, as might be your perception. Maybe it's time we drive back."

"First, we're going to have dinner, perhaps at the same place since it was so good, and then go to the park museum to view the volcano erupting as it gets dark."

Dinner proved even better than lunch, leaving us with a very good memory of that little restaurant, and by the time we arrived at the Thomas A. Jaggar Museum the sun had set. We joined the small crowd on the observation deck watching the fairly distant eruption, clearly visible from the bright yellowish glow and tendrils of flaming lava that from time to time shot up. Even at such a distance, the primordial power inspires the mind, and might I even say, "soul." Satisfied with the view, soon to be only memories, we entered the adjacent museum going from one information board to the next.

I'm feeling too tired to really absorb all the information, and it seems that Aminta feels the same as she doesn't really appear to be paying attention. Deciding to end our day at the volcano I expressed, "I think we've seen and experienced enough today. I'm feeling tired, and it's a long drive back in the dark."

"I agree, it's been a long day, although one of the best I can recall." Looking around she added, "So much interesting information here but we're too tired to absorb it."

"Unfortunately, you're right. My mind started drifting off as I read some of the plaques. Let's go."

Returning to the observation deck I'm feeling somewhat lightheaded and detached, like the world around me is different. Maybe it's just tiredness from such a long day, or my mind giving me a break from all the information.

Looking at the glowing volcano one more time the key erupted into my mind: INFORMATION! The common element of all that I've encountered is information—Religions generate mountains of information filling countless books, scrolls, and temples, while characterizing numerous cultures in the process. Religions are really information generating entities!

Grabbing Aminta's shoulder I exclaimed, "I've got it! The most important thing that religions have in common is information. I'm saturated with it, and have been trying to sort out the meaning, all along not appreciating that it's the information itself that stands out."

"Wow, that's a really unique angle. I've never viewed it in that way, but religions do generate vast amounts of information. All the Gods and Goddesses, stories about them, ways of worshipping the deities, the list goes on and on. It really never ends, as followers keep generating more."

"Right, such as creating different sects, and interpretations."

"When you think about it science also generates enormous amounts of information, and the fact that both do so offers a way to merge them."

"I think that I, or maybe I should say, "we," have hit on it."

"It was your notion and your odyssey, but I'm so happy to help."

Prior to the museum, I was not at all relishing the idea of driving back, but with the revelation I'm feeling completely invigorated. As we pulled into the hotel parking lot a few hours later a thought came to mind that tired me—Even if information is the common and key aspect, what does it really mean, and how can it merge religion and science beyond both sharing information as a feature? The wave of tiredness told me that the answer will have to wait. Despite our attraction for each other, we both fell asleep right after undressing and slipping under the sheets, sleep trumping romance.

Eager to see Volcanoes National Park from the air, as the website advertised, and also the entire island around the coast, we booked a helicopter tour online during breakfast. Fortunately, window seats, reserved upon booking, are available for the 11:00 o'clock flight. Even better, this tour includes a stop to see natural sites few get to experience. Arriving at the airport, I'm feeling a twinge of sadness thinking of when we will have to leave, and head back to reality living separate lives. These thoughts faded as we entered the helicopter office and started on the paperwork.

Due to the weight distribution, most likely, I'm seated beside the pilot. Aminta gave me her camera since photos will probably turn out better from my position. With the noise, and headset communication shared by all aboard, we couldn't really talk to each other anyways. As we lifted off and followed the western coast southwards, the notion of information popped into my mind. Everything I'm seeing is information, the highway we just travelled on, the Kailua-Kona tourist area, the Captain Cook memorial, the coffee plantations, hardened lava flows, and rift in the ground from an ancient earthquake. It also strikes me that some of this information is more permanent and stable, such as the hardened lava flows extending to the sea, and others more transient like the cars passing along the highway.

Crossing the lip of the active crater, who's glowing image triggered my revelation last night, I really appreciate the way that information presents itself at different rates, because whereas the crater rim seems etched in stone, literally, the flowing lava below us presents a much more dynamic picture, it changing every fraction of a second, even with bursts of fire from superheated sections. I feel the heat from it on my feet and legs, once again new and rapidly changing information. So absorbed in this new information perspective, and mesmerized by the primordial lava flow below the circling helicopter, I almost forgot to take pictures. Snapping out of it, I took the photos Aminta would want, each capturing a bit of the information flow. Yes, information does seem to be flowing with the lava.

During the journey onwards to Hilo and up the eastern coast, I barely paid attention to the monotone presentation of the pilot given my altered perspective. More information from him, and also from the sights. It's amazing how a concept can result in an entirely new way of viewing things. Each valley, waterfall within it, and opening to the ocean, information. Nature creates information as do people. Excited to share this insight with Aminta, I felt relieved when the pilot brought the machine down on a plateau by the sea.

Stretching our legs, we walked to a tall and narrow waterfall cascading down the cliff face. "What do you see, Aminta?"

"I see water falling."

"Of course, but beyond that what is really there?"

"What do you mean?"

"Each droplet of water, the mist, contact of the waterfall with the rocks, all information. Same with the rocks in the cliff face, and in the little stream at the bottom here. Some information changes faster than others, such as the water falling compared to the rocks, but all experience change as with the rocks continually wearing down."

"So, it's not just religions and science that produce information."

"Right, if it exists it creates information."

"And humans are really good at doing so, given our brain power."

"Very good point. Ultimately, I suppose, everything must be information, and what varies is the flow rate."

"And that relates to the permanence aspect, such as the information in those petroglyphs enduring, and this flow of water, or our conversation, less so."

"Or is it?" The question popped out, coming from my unconscious I suppose.

The rest of the flight passing from the wet eastern side of the island to the much drier northern coast, and then down the Kohala coast back to the airport, seems like a blur. I sense that the question I last asked, as much to myself as to Aminta, is pivotal to the ultimate answer, although how I'm not so sure. Maybe all the information is permanent in some way, much like the Anishinaabe notion of the spirit of all things persisting. What this might really mean is that information persists. My quest now is to see how feasible this all is.

The next day we made the transition from the King Kamehameha to the Hapuna Beach Prince Hotel, by where else, Hapuna Beach. Although we really enjoyed our time at the King Kamehameha and the Kailua-Kona area, Hapuna Beach is that of glossy travel magazines, a long stretch of soft light sand, gentle waves, and bikini clad beauties, one of them now being Aminta. After getting our room in the upper tier, discounted enough that we can afford a few nights, we made the journey through the multi-level hotel to the beach, strolling along to the end. Try as I might I cannot stop looking at everything as information; the beach and even all the grains of sand, water lapping on the shore, the beach chairs, umbrellas, hotel above. It's actually quite a disorientating, although very enlightening, perspective.

That night I think I took the perspective too far. While Aminta reclined on the bed after dinner, a flying cockroach, and yes, the heavenly paradise of Hawaii does have them, landed in her cleavage. In a panicked voice she shouted, "Get it off, quick!"

Thinking it's only a moth I laughed saying, "Maybe it's a male, who can blame him. Yet another piece of information."

The hand strike against my chest communicated information—She's pissed! Motivated to be more attentive, I reached over and grabbed the insect, throwing it across the floor. Walking over I discovered it's no moth. A rolled up promotional magazine, quick strike, and no more bug, but does the information about it persist? I fear this perspective will drive me crazy unless I work it all out, a strong motivation to persevere.

Almost needless to say, romance was not on Aminta's agenda for the evening after her encounter with the flying cockroach. All I got is, "We have to keep the screen door closed. I'm going to sleep." This is our first point of friction, but I think a short one, or restricted piece of information.

The next couple of days consisted of a drive across the island and along the eastern coast to Hilo, seeing some of the sites like Akaka Falls the first day, and then a drive around the northern coast and hike down into Pololu Valley on the northeastern coast on the second day. I read that the ancient Hawaiians colonized these valleys, the lush vegetation providing crops and fruit, waterfalls fresh water, and the sea a good source of protein in the form of fish. An idyllic life, other than for the occasional tsunami that could wipe out a valley.

While hiking into the Pololu Valley, I decided to talk about my evolving perspective to help move it ahead. "As you know I'm now obsessed with this information thing, and think that somehow it all persists."

"Hopefully that flying cockroach won't."

"The bug's body will decay, but the information about it and the encounter with your breasts might be permanent in some way."

"Did you really have to use that example?"

"Why does it bug you?"

Another hand strike against my chest. "You seem to like hitting." The smile ensured she realizes I'm joking.

"If you raise the bug thing anymore, you'll find out."

"All kidding aside, I do think that somehow there is permanence of the information about things, such as the seashore here." We had just reached the bottom of the trail. Walking along a path deeper into the valley we arrived at a marshy area, preventing further passage. "Also about the structure of this valley, like the marsh, and all the grass and plants growing in it."

"And like with us and this conversation, and unfortunately the bug incident."

"Exactly."

"Do you mean that it all goes to some heaven or place?"

"I don't know where it goes or how it gets there, but feel strongly that it does. It's like the revelation about information, now part two of it."

"You know, this is how science and religion might really merge, because you're proposing persistence of everything including what we do, all the information we generate, which is kind of religious. However, only science can answer how that might actually transpire."

"How's your physics?"

"Sorry, not so much information to provide with that."

"It wasn't my favorite subject either, but I'm more motivated for it now."

"That's the next step of your quest then."

A much more romantic evening than the night of the flying cockroach incident ended our time on the "Big Island," and as sad as the departure is, we have a couple of days on Oahu.

Staying at the historic Moana Surfrider, right on Waikiki Beach, brought the notion of permanence of information home, with all the historic photos on the second floor of the lobby. I realize that in a way photographs create a somewhat permanent record of the information, such as the young people on the beach a hundred or so years ago. Sad, and also inspiring in that although they're forever gone, there is persistence of the information about them.

On the hike to the top of Diamond Head the first morning after our arrival, I thought of how each step we're taking, every view, the sweat from the exertion, our thoughts, all the sounds, might somehow be permanent, the information preserved, recorded in some way. Now that's more of a motivation to do good in life than the Ten Commandments and the like!

On our last full day, we went surfing hiring an instructor for an hour. A bit wild with his loud voice and cross-eyed look, he gave us all the information we needed to get started, and made sure we succeeded with guidance on the water. As Aminta got up and rode the wave in, I noted the many gazes from both men and women. Appreciating how attractive, smart, and obviously athletic she is, I vocalized, "Ya, she's good."

Going with our instructor's advice, I paddled with the wave, making sure to look forward towards the shore as I got up, and not down at the board or water. Riding the wave is so exhilarating, going along with the flow and power, until it collapses. Although too immersed in the experience to ponder it, the notion of the wave and it collapsing stuck with me, as did the pain in my lower ribs from contact with the surfboard.

That evening over our meal on the outside terrace of the Moana Surfrider restaurant, I ventured, "The surfing today gave me an idea, or maybe more of a recall of physics." Not getting any reaction from her I continued, "There's this notion in quantum physics called collapse of the wave function. I recall that in the realm of the very small, or quantum world, different states can exist at the same time, but with an observation, as in an experiment, only one of the states manifests, the one that the experiment interacts with. It is said that the wave function for that state collapses, and is registered in the experiment."

Holding my hand while smiling warmly she replied, "You're talking Greek to me."

Smiling in return at her humor, I responded, "You speak Greek, so you get the idea."

"Somewhat, but maybe you can clarify."

"Okay, say a particle has an up and down state. These states are both present at the same time in the quantum world, and are described as waves. If the experiment detects the up state, the wave for that one collapses and is registered."

"What happens to the down state?"

"No one knows from what I understand, but it might disappear, phase into the up one, or maybe still occur in some other dimension."

"That's weird."

"The quantum world is indeed weird but revealing."

"I'm not sure what it has to do with your quest."

"I think it plays a role in the persistence of information, but I'm not sure how, since there can't be any collapse of the wave function at our macro level, only at the quantum level. One thing that made me think of this and information, besides the wave collapsing under me while surfing, is how information is preserved at the quantum level from what I remember. It might be a way that all this information persists."

"But how?"

"That's the next step in my quest—To put this together."

"We're at the end of our trip, so let's enjoy the night. How about putting this stuff aside for now and making some stimulating information together, something that will really persist?"

"I think we will persist; we really are great together."

"Yes, I'm sure as well, although tomorrow you're flying to British Columbia and I'm going to Los Angeles and onwards to Greece, so it will have to be in spirit for now."

We did create stimulating information well into the night, not wanting to let the moment pass, but pass it did, as it always does. I wonder if our experiences together are etched into the cosmos somehow, and not like a two-dimensional image, but as the actual experience we had together, every feeling, thought, word, and action. It's a pleasing notion and one that might well be true.

IMMORTALITY ACTUALIZED

The warmth of Oahu to the cold of Revelstoke British Columbia in winter, quite a change. The best available locum turned out to be in this mecca of skiing and also snowmobiling, or sledding as those devoted to the activity like to say. The town of Revelstoke, like so many in British Columbia, arose in conjunction with railway expansion in the 1800's, the town named after Lord Revelstoke, a major financier. The quaint railway museum right in town alongside the railway tracks, does a great job of depicting this history, showcasing actual trains from that era. With the photos, intact machinery, and information plaques, the times are then preserved in a very real sense.

I'm fortunate in at least two ways, the first being the great skiing at Revelstoke Mountain, with more vertical than Whistler, very challenging runs, and far less in the way of lift lines. After the "horror" I avoided skiing, but will now be returning to the sport I love so much. The second is that a young radiologist, also doing a locum, has a background in physics and loves to ski.

Not wanting to rely entirely on another person's knowledge for such an important, at least to me, quest, I started researching information pertaining to my notion that everything might persist in some form, and likely tied into the process of wave function collapse. Yes, a heavy topic but information is out there about it, and not all of it in an indecipherable form. My readings confirm that collapse of the wave function is restricted to the quantum realm, or in other words, that which we cannot see. It does not apply to entities such as people. This could be a challenge for my idea, and where James, my new friend, comes in handy. My second time on the slopes he came along, and having the gondola car to ourselves, I thought this is the time to test his knowledge.

"This might not seem like a real ski topic, but I'm curious about something in physics, and recall you saying you have a PhD in it, I suppose it helping for radiology."

"It seemed like a natural extension to go into radiology with my background, even though most do not have much in the way of a physics background. What are you curious about?"

"I've been reading about wave function collapse, and I know it occurs at the micro quantum level, but is there any way it could pertain to the macro level?"

"That's an interesting question, because physicists often treat quantum processes as if they do not relate at all to this macro world, but everything in nature is interconnected so they must. Quantum computing comes to mind, there now being a great deal of interest and funding for it. A limitation of current computers is that they can only handle so much information at a given time, but quantum computing allows virtually unlimited information to occur at one point in time, each piece a quantum state. The problem is that any interaction with the information causes that state to collapse and the others to disappear."

"So, an interaction is like when a traditional wave function collapse experiment measures a state?"

"Exactly, it's not just an experimental measurement but any interaction. If computer engineers can design a system such that the information is kept viable until the one piece is required, then the speed of computing goes way up, sort of like comparing horse and buggy to a jet fighter."

"That's definitely an example of the quantum realm applying to the macro world."

"It's one of many, because all the microscopic atoms and molecules within us operate according to quantum processes, while playing a key role in the form characterizing us, and even though they act differently they express themselves in this realm."

"So how might quantum wave function collapse work at a macro level?"

"It doesn't, but the macro form, such as your body and inquisitive mind at a given moment, are derived from billions, or more likely trillions, of micro quantum processes, and these can experience collapse of the wave function."

Excited I now pictured how it could work, "And the constellation or summation of quantum wave function collapses provides for the macro form at a given time!"

"Yes, it could work in that way, although less open minded physicists might well reject the notion, only to be using a quantum computer in however many years."

"When I move my little finger slightly, numerous quantum, let's say potential states, precede it. Then with the collapse of certain ones the finger motion materializes."

"Right, each collapsed quantum wave function represents a very micro component of the finger movement, some for the skin, others for muscles, tendons, blood vessels, cells, and the like, and also the way each behaves with the movement. It's kind of like an orchestra where each musician contributes, and with each musician numerous actions occur to produce their particular sound. Micro to macro."

"Each of those potential states, or more exactly the collapse of the one that is actualized, represents a piece of information."

"I've never thought of it in that way, but yes. Even the ones that do not collapse are information in a sense, just different in that they are only potential, not actualized. The potential states that collapse represent actualized form or expressions, and so the information is more robust."

"Given that information is supposed to be preserved at a quantum level, does this mean that the actualized state persists?"

"Wow, that's quite the notion, and I don't see why not. Of course, the macro form cannot, as with your finger movement. It's gone right when you complete the motion, but a trace of sorts consisting of the constellation of micro wave function collapses of potential states, into the actualized finger motion, could, although where I do not know."

"It must be in the quantum realm somewhere, in what I might take the liberty of referring to as a quantum actualization record."

Considering it briefly James expressed, "Actualization of certain potential states recorded at a quantum level, in your quantum actualization record. It makes sense because the potential states occur at a quantum level, so why wouldn't the ones that collapse into actualized states be recorded at a quantum level?"

"So it's possible?"

"Yes, I believe that it is."

Our absorption in the conversation and discovery almost resulted in a return journey to the bottom. Only the bouncing of the cable car with its arrival at the station and doors automatically opening alerted us. Scrambling to collect our gear we quickly exited. An alert attendant seeing us struggle helped by taking our skis. "You guys need to wake up, maybe less partying and more coffee!"

"Sorry, we're awake, just distracted."

"I'll say."

As we skied down mogul runs, some with trees and others open, I tried to visualize all the micro quantum potential states, and how only certain ones are actualized with the particular turn made and direction taken. The macro form in effect a constellation of countless actualized micro quantum states. Talk about seeing the world differently!

As the runs and day progressed I began to appreciate how my new perspective applies to time, or the passage of it. Thinking in terms of future, present, and past, it seems logical that the future consists of all the potential states, only varying in probability. For instance, while on this chairlift, the potentiality of it continuing to the top in the next minute is greater than it stopping, but that one is also quite probable. Way down in probability is the chairlift falling to the ground. I recall hearing a physics saying that anything that is not impossible is possible. If an occurrence does not violate the laws of the universe it can potentially occur, but only certain potential scenarios are highly probable for a given set of circumstances. The present must be the very brief moment when potential states are converted into actualized events. Hence, when the chairlift continues onwards and upwards that potential scenario is actualized. It is brief, because there is no way of undoing what actually occurs even a second or two into it. Once the chairlift continues on, it can't be erased. The actualized potential states comprise the past, entering into what I'm referring to as the quantum actualization record. This record only contains occurrences that have been actualized.

Satisfied with my new understanding of time, and also feeling hungry and tired from both the physical and mental exertion, I suggested we ski all the way to the bottom and have lunch on the outdoor patio, given that the sun is out and it's not that cold. James agreed and we actualized the series of potentialities associated with skiing to the bottom, entering the restaurant, getting a table outside, and ordering lunch.

Seeing me smiling he asked, "Did I miss the joke?"

"No, it's not a joke, just a very different way of looking at the world, and passage of time." I proceeded to share my revelation about the nature of time.

"It fits well with the notion of multiple micro quantum states being actualized when an event occurs in the macro realm." Pausing seemingly lost in thought he added, "You've really got me intrigued by all this and I'm thinking of various implications, of which there are several. First, though, I'll be the devil's advocate and present a view that might work against yours: Some physicists argue that there is no time at all, everything just existing. Julian Barbour, who's quite the character and thinker like you, is best known for this perspective. He believes that all that we know is just present as kind of a landscape, with the most probable events more strongly represented in the landscape. According to this perspective, continuing up the chairlift when we're on it is very strongly represented, as it has the highest probability under the circumstances. Based on his "end of time" concept, the future, present, and past just occur as a static entity. It somewhat aligns with how the future and past are commonly viewed as places we can just time travel to."

"That's a weird perspective on time, though, with future, present, and past all just occurring with no clear separation."

"Very, and the concept is really only based upon interpretations of certain equations, particularly ones pertaining to relativity theory. A critique of the "end of time" perspective is that complex equations commonly yield unrealistic and implausible solutions, and they should not be over-interpreted. In addition, certain time-based sequences of events, such as how we process information cast doubt on this notion. Just be aware though that if it's true your perspective might not hold up."

"Although, if it's all a static landscape, the three time scenarios—the future as potentialities, the present actualization of certain potentialities, and the past a record of the actualized occurrences—likely did transpire at some point, and the static landscape of time just records the events and probabilities associated with them. Maybe this is how the quantum actualization record of the past works?"

"You are good at reasoning this out."

"Thanks, as are you. I'm glad that the actualization of this locum included meeting you."

"I'm glad we met as well, great mind expanding conversation and skiing. However, I suspect you would have actualized the potentiality of connecting with someone else with a physics background, so seemingly strong is your motivation to actualize the potentiality of working this out."

"You might be right, but you also have an open mind which I need at this point."

"Speaking of an open mind, there are very intriguing implications of your perspective."

"Such as?"

"One has to do with the static time notion that seemingly counters your view."

"What are you considering?"

"When we say that macro form arises from a constellation of micro quantum wave function collapses, what we're really saying is that "stitched" together discrete quantum states provide for a continuous form at a macro level."

"I'm not sure I follow."

"Future potentialities are separate quantum states as wave functions, at least as we're reasoning it out, right?"

"Yes."

"When a macro entity interacts with quantum states, numerous discrete wave functions collapse, and in the process link or stitch together to produce the fabric or form of the macro entity. Since this form is based on linked micro states it is continuous, while the underlying quantum states are discrete, like a blanket derived from numerous individual stitches. Take the finger movement we talked about earlier—The quantum wave functions relating to all aspects of a given motion collapse when the matter-energy of the finger interacts with them, and the constellation of these quantum states, representing the given movement, in a sense link or stitch together producing the macro form of the ongoing finger motion. That motion is continuous and smooth based on the linking together of multiple discrete quantum wave function collapses."

"That makes sense but what does it have to do with a static time?"

"Equations derived from relativity theory produce time lacking any clear distinctions; it just exists without future, present, or past, and so is continuous. Quantum theory, the other major contending view for how the universe, or at least time, is structured, argues for discrete aspects to time. Due to this seemingly insurmountable difference the theories never merge. However, if we follow the same general reasoning as with the actualization of potentialities process, there is a way: Maybe time or the fabric of it is "stitched" together from countless discrete quantum states, with the form of time emerging as continuous, whereas it really has a discrete basis at a very fine level. The same applies to space and therefore space-time. Hence, processes related to space-time, such as gravity, emerge as smooth and continuous, while the underlying quantum reality is discrete."

"And this discrete basis provides for time distinctions when viewed from the perspective of potentialities being actualized via matter-energy interactions, to form a record of actualized events."

"Indeed. You know, for someone without a background in physics you're picking up on it fast. Let's see how you do with the next implication dealing with time travel. I'll start by saying that your idea aligns with what has been found."

"Time travel has been discovered?" I'd never heard of such an occurrence outside of science fiction.

"Yes, there is one proven form known as time dilation. To set this up it's important to appreciate how space and time go together as space-time. In physics many concepts are connected, such as momentum and angular momentum, and space-time. The speed of light is in a sense the product or result of multiplying space and time, meaning that if you travel through space close to the speed of light, there is nothing really left for time, and it slows."

"So that's what's meant when they say that time slows or stops at the speed of light."

"Yes, but nothing with any mass can achieve the speed of light, so there's always something left over for time. Now with time dilation, a person we'll say, leaves the planet Earth on a very speedy spacecraft and travels through space close to the speed of light. Let's ignore the fact that no biological organism would likely survive acceleration to the speed of light. Given that this person is experiencing very little in the way of time passing, he or she barely ages. Meanwhile, millions of years are passing for those stuck back on Earth travelling far below the speed of light. When the person returns to Earth, and the spacecraft slows to Earth speed, everyone that person knew prior to leaving the planet are long gone, and who knows, maybe dinosaurs have evolved again."

"Time has been dilated."

"Exactly."

"But how does that relate to my perspective?"

"Ah, very nicely. According to what you're suggesting there can never be any time travel to the future, at least your own, because it's not there other than for potential states, nor to the past, given that it's already actualized; it's now in the form of a record of sorts. If a person ever traveled to the future of potentialities, then it would no longer be the future, just the present, as certain ones would be actualized by the time traveler's presence. Returning to the past cannot occur as the past is done, there are no potential states anymore. With time dilation, the only viable form of time travel, a person can never go to their own future or past, nor to anyone else's past. It is restricted to another person's future, as long as the time traveler leaves the planet and travels close to the speed of light. If they remain connected to the other person, such as by remaining on the planet, they are entangled, and cannot be separated in space-time. In that scenario time dilation cannot occur. Therefore, your view aligns with what is viable in terms of time travel."

"I like your explanation, and can see how the perspective aligns with realistic, not science fiction, time travel. What about other implications?"

"Maybe a set of them in that the universe seems to be structured to ensure that potential states are always actualized." Noting my puzzled look, he explained, "We already looked at how no body with mass can achieve the speed of light, a scenario where there is no longer any passage through time. For potential states to be actualized there must be some component of time as in a forward progression, and if time ceases this cannot occur. However, given that no body with mass can reach the speed of light, time progression always occurs ensuring that potential states continue to be actualized, although maybe at a much slower speed as in time dilation.

Likewise, for potential states to be actualized there must be space, as how could anything exist if there is no space at all? The linkage of space and time ensures that there is always space for potential states to be actualized. Then there is the fact that absolute zero temperature cannot be achieved, which aligns in that if this was to occur everything subjected to it ceases activity of any sort, meaning that potential states cannot be actualized. Finally, there is entropy or how order proceeds to disorder. For example, a new car ages; an old car does not spontaneously improve. In the absence of any interactions that can actualize potential states, order naturally proceeds to disorder, ensuring that some potential state—greater disorder—is actualized."

"So, everything in the universe ensures that potential states will always be actualized?"

"It appears so, and it also appears that our lunch is coming. We need it for all the brain power, not to mention leg power, we're using up."

With food for needed energy, and a coffee for me, beer for James, he expressed, "A very powerful and kind of odd implication of your view just came to me."

"And that is?"

"First, what do you think your view of the present, where potential occurrences are actualized, says about the world around us?"

"I'm not following you?"

"Okay, the world we know consists of matter and energy, as paired states like with space-time. Matter-energy interacting with quantum wave functions representing future potentialities, is really what actualize certain potential states. The form of matter-energy is itself derived from a constellation of these quantum wave function collapses. For example, when I reach for my beer and touch the glass, the matter-energy of my hand movement interacts with the future quantum potentialities, and those representing ongoing contact of my hand with the glass collapse, ensuring the macro form of my hand remaining on the glass."

Continuing with his line of thought I added, "The macro form in turn influences the probability associated with further potential quantum wave functions, such that if you touch the glass, the probability for all the potential quantum states representing further contact of your hand on the glass rise, while the probability for those representing other options diminish."

"Correct, and whatever potential scenario is actualized enters into your quantum actualization record. But, what does this say about the permanence of matter-energy?"

Thinking it over I replied, "It can really only exist in the present, because there are only potential states in the future and the quantum actualization record in the past. Wow, that's really odd. All this around us is then only occurring in the present moment!"

"Right, and it follows because although we know there was a mountain here say last year, that same mountain with all the trees, leaves, animals, rocks, and the like exactly the same is gone, except in the quantum actualization record. Think of the photos presented in the media showing glaciers receding with global warming. When put in chronological order we see the glacier retreating, but we can't actually see the glacier as it was back then, except for the photograph."

"Ah, but the photo stays the same."

"No, because the paper and chemicals are undergoing change, and even at a very fine level change occurs in seconds. Entropy alone will ensure that the photo changes, and we can't see the prior photo, as it's gone."

"It makes sense James, and reminds me of the Buddhist notion that nothing has any permanence in this world; the only thing that is permanent is change."

"You've really got me rolling now, and not down the slopes. I have an idea that might or might not apply, but it could explain an interesting entity known as dark matter: It's matter, or matter-energy, that we cannot detect because it doesn't interact with the matter-energy we're familiar with. However, it actually comprises the vast majority of the matter in the universe, based on results of gravitational studies. Let's assume that the matter we're familiar with only exists in the present moment to actualize potential states. If so, then what supports it?"

Seeing exactly what my clever new friend is getting at, I jumped at the answer, "Dark matter, and since it doesn't interact with the matter we're used to it can't actualize potential states! Also, given the support or scaffolding role, and permanence, you'd expect it to be far more abundant than the matter-energy only found in the present moment."

"Exactly. Theorizing can be a lot of fun, and revealing, although we have to appreciate that it's speculative."

"Of course, but we may have hit on a discovery of enormous significance."

"I'm sure we have, and enormous is an understatement, because the quantum actualization record will be the ultimate discovery. Actually, it will be a treasure, and of far greater value than what all the discoveries and treasures in our history combined are worth!"

"How do you figure that?"

"Consider the information that the quantum actualization record will reveal—Everything that has happened in the universe!"

"Your right, as long as the occurrence is actualized information, it's in the record. Of course, it can't say anything about the brief present moment or future."

"The information is restricted to the past, containing everything that has happened."

Seeing a potential flaw, I expressed, "From what I understand of physics, clearly less than you, time is relative to the observer, so how do we say that the past of everyone and everything is in the quantum actualization record?"

"Good point, but if an event is actualized it's in there. A grain of sand that has moved on a planet across the universe, what we just said, it's all in the quantum actualization record. If entities are entangled, like us talking on this planet, then we are actualizing potential occurrences at the same time and rate to all extents and purpose, but if we were to separate, such as me on a spaceship travelling near the speed of light, then I will actualize events including the aging of my body much slower, and the passage of time will be different; recall the time dilation we discussed. However, regardless of all that, once a potential occurrence is actualized it enters into the record."

"So, information about everything that has happened in the universe is sitting there, waiting to be discovered!"

"Amazing isn't it, and there's another implication, this one for space travel. Distances in space are vast, such as thousands, millions, and even billions of light years. Research looking at planets around suns strongly suggests great potential for other intelligent life forms, and there are almost certainly numerous civilizations in the universe, although our egos often influence us to think we are the only advanced beings."

"I agree and concur with your perspective regarding how entitled humans tend to be. It's ludicrous to think that we're the only ones."

"Then there is the likelihood of many universes. Anyway, from a perspective of space travel in ours, how can we possibly do it given the distances involved?"

"What about time warps, wormholes, and the like."

"As we discussed, the only form of time travel that seems viable is time dilation, and that only allows you to travel to someone else's future, so long as you separate from the other person, travel through space near the speed of light, and return to the same place, in which case they have aged radically compared to you, although both of you have aged. Wormholes and time warps are theoretical possibilities, but not practical. For example, wormholes between different regions of space-time might be feasible, but as time lengthens the "bridge" thins such that no entity with mass can use it. In other words, the bridge will break if time travel is attempted. Despite science fiction popularity, it appears that time travel to your own past or future, or someone else's past is impossible, aligning with our perspective."

"And I recall that you mentioned no biological organism will likely survive acceleration to the speed of light, or close even, I suppose."

"Yes, that is one major problem with space travel, because if distances are typically in hundreds to billions of light years, and nothing can go faster or warp time for rapid time travel, how can we possibly travel to far off planets, and meet other intelligent beings?" Pausing and smiling he added, "Of course, not quite as smart as us."

"Of course. I've often wondered that too, because people talk as if we just get on a ship, go into suspended animation keeping us alive but slowing aging, and then wake up at the destination, but really?"

"Well exactly. There are many problems, such as is it even viable to "freeze" a body and slow the aging process? Then there's the issue of the time frame with some aging occurring. Radiation in space is another major concern as it damages nervous system components resulting in impaired ability to think clearly, a real problem when we're considering long range space travel. Also, assuming that we could survive acceleration to near the speed of light, a collision with a speck of dust would be like a nuclear explosion, meaning no more ship. Given this reality and the fact that we almost certainly will not be able to survive acceleration to near the speed of light, we will have to travel much slower. What that means is that hundreds of light years, a very short distance in the universe, becomes thousands or millions of years, and with some aging, the space travelers even if in suspended animation, will be dead upon arrival."

"Therefore, long range space travel is likely unrealistic?"

Skipping over the largely rhetorical question, James expressed, "But then there is your quantum actualization record. If we can access it and learn how to read it, the lives of beings right across the universe will be evident!"

"And in every detail because the information covers everything, including actions, feelings, thoughts, dreams, all that the organism has every actualized. We could learn everything that other beings have discovered and know intimate details about them without even leaving the planet!"

"We can even communicate because whatever is actualized, like a thought about them, is in the record. I conjure up an image, and once actualized other beings can "see" it. Kind of like the ultimate social media."

Considering the implications, I ventured, "The discovery and use of the quantum actualization record might be a kind of litmus test for the intelligence and advanced standing of beings, in that those who get the idea and discover it join the universe club, while those that persist in "space travel," don't."

"Very good point, and I bet that's right."

Another notion came to mind, related to my medical background. "Meeting beings from another planet in person would also be very risky, due to biological contamination. A virus that we barely notice could wipe out those from another world lacking any immunity at all. Hence, there will be a huge safety factor in only using the quantum actualization record."

"Yes, and let's not forget our propensity for aggression and conquest, or that of other intelligent beings. Safety is a real plus of utilizing information contained in the quantum actualization record, and as you mentioned, almost certainly a litmus test of intelligence and sophistication."

"This is so amazing."

"I feel the same, and might I suggest that you write a book about it." Smiling he added, "Just include an acknowledgment of the amazing role your friend James played."

"Will do."

Moving from intense mental to physical activity, we returned to the slopes, taking on the most challenging runs, the revelations seemingly energizing both of us. Extending the day to the very last run, we drove back into town as darkness started to set in, a stark contrast to the light of our insight. In my apartment, I suddenly realized that even though my knowledge of the science aspect has ramped up massively, and I now have a viable scenario, I'm still not entirely clear about how religion fits into it all. Too tired to think it through I decided to discuss it with Aminta tomorrow, particularly given how helpful she has been in the discovery, and her informed take on religion.

My shift starting after lunch, I called Aminta following breakfast when I knew her work day in Europe will be ending, given the time difference. We faced timed adding a more personal touch to the conversation.

"So how is your quest coming, my lover?"

"I'm so fortunate because based on a discussion with a new colleague and friend here with a background in physics, James, I've got it."

"That's great, tell me about it."

Feeling confident in the discovery, I relayed everything to her.

Listening patiently and absorbing it fully, she responded, "It does fit together well, and the implications are so amazing. You are fortunate for having that friend. Is that it then, the end of your odyssey?"

"No, one thing remains, and part of the reason I called."

Feigning disappointment, she intervened, "You mean that it wasn't just to hear my nice voice and see my lovely face?"

"Mostly, but I also want you to help with the final piece—How this knowledge merges religion and science."

"Yes, I see what you mean, but it appears to be quite straightforward."

"Perhaps I burned too much brain and body energy yesterday with the thinking and skiing; I'm just not seeing it yet."

"Okay, what do all religions generate?" Answering her own question, she continued, "The common element, information. As we discussed, mountains of information about each one, and where does this end up?"

"In the quantum actualization record, of course."

"Right, so religions add to this record, wherever it is, and given how religious we seem to be as a species, religious information forms a large portion of our contribution."

"But is that really merging the two? In a sense, yes, but it's then almost like information going into a digital record for the universe, and not some powerful connection."

"Maybe you and James are being too scientific by assuming that the quantum actualization record is restricted to one universe."

Catching her drift, I replied, "Theoretically more than one universe exists, and if so why couldn't the quantum actualization record contain information about all of them, at least actualized potentialities?"

"It is likely, assuming that the actualization of potentialities process is true."

"So not only the universe, but what lies beyond is ultimately comprised of information at the finest level!"

"Again, your science focus might be getting in the way, because you're making it seem like, how do you say, a static entity, as a digital record."

"You're right, it's not a static entity, but a very dynamic organic one, always growing and changing, evolving in a sense, with each new piece of information pertaining to actualized events, including religious knowledge."

"That's better, a more flexible perspective that captures what is going on."

"Yes, I see it now, very dynamic. Each universe might really be an information generating system where potential scenarios are actualized, based on constellations of micro quantum wave function collapses. The information about these actualized potentialities continually passes into the quantum actualization record ever changing it." An extra thought coming to mind I added, "And to ensure that this very active process continues, each universe must have space and time, or space-time to be accurate."

"The whole thing is very interconnected, each part working together, like occurs in nature."

"Space-time enables matter-energy to do its thing actualizing potential occurrences, and conversely, space-time is difficult to imagine without the ongoing actualization of potentialities, since this process occupies space and occurs over time. The information generated adds to the quantum actualization record. Indeed, a very symbiotic process."

"As occurs in biology, that you are so familiar with, both from your medical background, and our time together."

"The latter is far more exciting."

"Yes, it is, and is that it then for your ideas?"

"Maybe, but I feel something is missing."

"You might be missing me and the associated biology."

"For sure, but I think this has more to do with the concept of God, or Gods and Goddesses in polytheistic systems."

Hesitating briefly, she commented, "I see what you mean, because the concept doesn't include them other than as information generated by religions."

Suddenly it came to me, undoubtedly helped along from the free flow of ideas occurring between us. "You're an expert on religions, or at least some."

"I'm not sure about that."

"Don't undervalue your knowledge, as it's there."

"Okay, and thanks."

"So, what do you think that God, or the summation of Gods and Goddesses in polytheistic systems, ultimately represent?"

Taking time to ponder the question, she responded, "All wisdom, knowledge." Pausing as the revelation came to her she continued, "All information!"

"Yes, the quantum actualization record as the dynamic entity you've helped me see it as, and not just a digital record, is the embodiment of all information. It's like an organism in that it's changing and growing, but is eternal consistent with a deity. From a perspective of religion, it is God or the summation of Gods and Goddesses."

"The Informative God."

"And that God actually merges science and religion, given that the scientific process of information generation provides for God!"

"I believe you've captured the essence of it. Religion and science do merge in this way, and I might add, also from how both help show the way forward."

"At least when not corrupted by political or profit motives."

"In a more ideal form, they can and often do help with social cohesion and proper care of the natural world."

"A very practical function of the information generated by both, that we can take advantage of right now."

"That's a real plus because it will take a while to discover the quantum actualization record." Pausing momentarily to collect her thoughts, Aminta added, "One thing still puzzling me, though, is does this God intervene, such as placing a protective barrier around you with "the horror" and the terrorist incident?"

"As a dynamic entity, we cannot say for sure, but taking a more scientific perspective, I doubt it. Much of what happens is random, part of the information generation we've talked about, and sometimes that randomness comes out in your favor and at other times not, and even both in a sense at the same time. Think of those events I experienced; neither was in my favor in the first place, but my reaction to them, based on my youth and strength, was. Given that it was my attributes that probably saved me, I can even say that overall I was unlucky, but compensated. For sure, if I was old at the time of both, I would have been finished."

"Many will still say that God intervened to ensure you completed your mission in life."

"Yes, I'm sure they will. However, I've come to learn that despite our outward presentation we are all very vulnerable emotionally, and certainly to the prospect of harm and death. To protect us emotionally there are our psychological defenses, that we talked about previously, including reassuring attributions and beliefs. It's comforting to believe that God is looking out for us, but the drawback here is when things do not go well we feel abandoned, or worse punished, and at our most vulnerable moments. Think of those unfortunate people who died on the bus; if they could comment I'm sure they would feel terribly let down by God if intervention is a real occurrence. I believe it's more to the point that we all take a journey based on circumstances, personal attributes, and yes random events, and that journey is how we become part of the body of the Informative God forever. Actually, quite the honor when you think about it, and one that ultimately compensates for the pain and suffering that life randomly hands out."

"That does make sense, and is very hopeful in that we all continue even after our brief presence here on this world ends."

"We continue with every aspect of our life; thoughts, dreams, fantasies, feelings, movements, reactions, embodied in the fabric of the cosmos. Immortality in a word!"

"Immortality actualized with the actualization of potentialities process."

"A very enlightened point, Aminta."

"Thanks, and to add another worthwhile point, the type of God you're describing is more believable than one, or multiple Gods and Goddesses, that seem to influence events in mostly unpredictable ways."

"And believable in that it has a solid scientific basis, so lacking with other versions."

"Do you think that this perspective will be acceptable to religious people?"

"That's up to the individual, but what people really seem to fear the most is losing who they are. It is the ultimate loss in many ways, since the "self" is what we are most familiar with. We wish for it to continue, but even highly religious people have their doubts about this. For example, do we go as who we are to heaven, or hell? If reincarnated, then we definitely lose the self, and even "soul" if you believe in Buddhism. With the Informative God notion, our entire life is preserved indefinitely."

"The "self" persists then, and there is no loss of it!"

"Exactly, and even though we do not live forever in a biological sense, we do indeed persist, providing a strong motivation to make a real effort in life."

"Actually, given how the whole process is so dynamic, maybe we can "live" forever in a sense"

"In what way, Aminta?"

"Okay, I will try to explain it—If the actualized events in a person's life are embodied forever in the Informative God, then as a static state it will just represent information preserved, right?"

"Yes, and I think I might by seeing what you're getting at."

"However, in a dynamic form this information is likely to be active ongoing."

"Meaning that the person will "relive" their life, or that actualized while they were alive!"

"Each person will "relive" it for eternity!"

"That's an incredible notion, Aminta, because then we really do preserve the self."

"Somewhat of a heaven for those who have a good life, although maybe a hell of sorts if life is short and painful."

"True, but even if it's the latter for a person, or any organism for that matter, at least it's a life." Pondering the revelation momentarily an implication came to me. "But how do we know if what we are experiencing is our actual life or a reliving of it?"

"Good question and I do not have a good answer; maybe we cannot tell."

"Wow, does this ever support the notion of living for experiences, because the more experiences you have in life the more intriguing the "reliving" of it will be."

"It definitely suggests that we all need to make the most of what we have."

"Related to that, it's best to minimize suffering to the self and others."

"Particularly considering that the "reliving" will be forever."

"Speaking of intriguing experiences to relive for eternity, perhaps we need to find a way to continue our odyssey."

"You mean add to information of the universe, and beyond, and be part of the Informative God as a couple?"

"I can't think of anything more enticing to relive forever."

"True, although there is your whole quest and the discovery, that I'm so glad to be part of."

Her words made me realize that my quest will indeed be recorded in the quantum actualization record, as part of the Informative God. All my experiences, feelings, and thoughts, part of something much bigger, embodied in the fabric of the cosmos to relive forever!

POSTSCRIPT

Session paused. Ancient Earth language translator still active.

The teacher looked at the reaction of his scholar in trust before speaking. "On this, the 100,000-year anniversary of the quantum actualization record first being suggested by one of our ancestors, it is very appropriate to experience the life of the one who proposed it."

"Yes very, and your advice in my studies has always been accurate. It is one thing to know about the history of the discovery, and another to experience this crucial segment of his life, and that of those who assisted him. As usual it feels like I just lived it myself."

"That is the power of the record as it provides every aspect of the life of those who are actualized. We can see what they are reliving, although our unique way of accessing it allows us to vary the rate of events and focus on select experiences. Meanwhile, the person "relives" all their experiences because everything that has been actualized is part of the "Informative God" that he gained insight about."

"It is an important life to relive, given the discovery made."

"If it were not for his insight and religion-scientists learning how to access the quantum actualization record 333 years later, we would not have survived. By learning from other intelligent life forms also at risk of self-destruction, we took the steps necessary to preserve life forms on Earth, and in the process our own species."

"From your instruction and my exposure to the record, I appreciate that intelligent life forms with any propensity to aggression, are very unlikely to survive and thrive over time unless they discover and learn to access the record."

"You have learned well my fine scholar. The record reveals the self-destruction of many intelligent life forms that failed to connect with the record."

"Should I learn more of his life?"

"Learning is always good, the spirit of curiosity and exploration, without locking your mind into a set way of thinking. That is something we discovered from the countless other intelligent life forms we came to know from the record, and our interactions, via the record of course, with those who also accessed it."

"It takes time, though, to cover segments of the record, even when accelerated, and I have other studies to commence. Might you tell me what happened in his life, as I know you have explored much of it?"

"He and his female friend Aminta went on to bond, in an ancient practice known as marriage; you might want to add it to your learning tasks. They both lived to an old age for that time. As you appreciate we now live much longer and in good health due to knowledge derived from the record, and our own medical discoveries. They had children, and he did write about the insight acknowledging all who helped, although it was largely ignored until perhaps a hundred years after, when attempts began to find the record."

"So, he never knew that it would lead to all this?"

"No, but my research covering the end of his life reveals that he passed on fully convinced that his life is embodied in something vast and powerful. I think he would not have been too surprised that a 100,000 years later you and I are experiencing the sequence leading to his insight."

"It is a very powerful story showing how we are all immortal in a very real sense."

"And one that reveals the power and permanence of information, and the merging of religion and science with the Informative God!"

www.ingramcontent.com/pod-product-compliance
Lightning Source LLC
LaVergne TN
LVHW051830080426
835512LV00018B/2795